L. B Brown

Biographical Sketches of the Governor, Councillors and Members

Of the Senate and House of Representatives of the New Hampshire:

Volume VII

L. B Brown

Biographical Sketches of the Governor, Councillors and Members
Of the Senate and House cf Representatives of the New Hampshire: Volume VII

ISBN/EAN: 9783337183783

Printed in Europe, USA, Canada, Australia, Japan

Cover: Foto ©ninafisch / ɼixelio.de

More available books at **www.hansebooks.com**

BIOGRAPHICAL SKETCHES

OF THE

GOVERNOR, COUNCILLORS,

AND MEMBERS OF THE

SENATE AND HOUSE OF REPRESENTATIVES

OF THE

EW HAMPSHIRE LEGISLATURE

FOR 1893-'94.

COMPILED BY L. B. BROWN.

VOLUME VII.

PRICE, TWENTY-FIVE CENTS.

CONCORD, N. H.:
H. B. BROWN, PUBLISHER.
1893.

Biographical Sketches

1893='94.

GOVERNOR.

JOHN BUTLER SMITH, of Hillsborough, is the son of Ammi and Lydia F. Smith, and was born at Rockingham, Vermont, April 12, 1838. He comes from sturdy Scotch-Irish stock, whose characteristics have been the strength and pride of the leading men and women of our state, and his New Hampshire origin is traced in the fact that he is descended from Lieut. Thomas Smith, who first settled in Chester, lived for a time in Londonderry and afterwards removed to New Boston; and his father Ammi was born in Acworth, removing to Vermont at the age of 33, and became a successful woolen manufacturer there. When John B. was nine years old his father removed to Hillsborough, where he lived until his death, in 1887.

The subject of this sketch received his early education in the public schools of the town and at Francestown academy where he excelled as a classical scholar, and at the age of 16 he was nearly fitted for college. He was led, however, to adopt a business career and after engaging in employment in Henniker, Manchester and New Boston, in 1863 he began business for himself by purchasing a drug store in Manchester, which he owned for a year, and then established a knit goods factory in the town of Washington. Subse-

quently he leased the Sawyer woolen mill at North Weare, and in 1866 he built at Hillsborough Bridge a small mill which was the beginning of the extensive knit goods factory now owned and operated by the Contoocook Mills Company, of which Mr. Smith is the president and principal owner. He continued his residence in Manchester for 17 years and has been a resident of Hillsborough since 1880, where he has lately erected a fine residence. His wife is Emma E., daughter of Stephen Lavender of Boston, and they have one son, their first born having died at the age of two years. Mr. Smith is a Congregationalist in religion and in politics has always been an earnest Republican, serving his party as a presidential elector in 1884 and as a member of the executive council in 1887-9, and he has always been active in the councils of his party. He has been strong, self-reliant, energetic, persistent and has achieved a wonderful success in the business world, having amassed a competence which enables him to give with a free hand to every good work that commends itself to his conscience and judgment. He is dignified, yet approachable and companionable, and is one of the true and solid men of the Old Granite State, whom the people delight to honor by official preferment.

COUNCIL.

District No. 1.—TRUE L. NORRIS, Portsmouth. Democrat, Episcopal, editor, married. Born in Manchester and educated in the public schools of New Hampshire and Massachusetts and fitted for Harvard college, but instead of entering college, he enlisted in the service of his country, serving in the 5th Massachusetts Vols. He afterwards read law in the office of his father, the late Col. A. F. L. Norris, in Boston, and was admitted to practice on the day he became of age. He practiced his profession in Boston for several years and then entered the newspaper profession, and for several years he represented the New York Herald, Boston Globe and Manchester Union in Concord. When Col. Charles A. Sinclair purchased the Daily Evening Times and Weekly States and Union in 1887, he went to Portsmouth and became editor and manager of both papers and has remained there until this time, where he has achieved a phenomenal success in building up these papers till they rank among the first in the state in circulation and influence. Col. Norris is a sagacious business man, of broad and liberal ideas; there isn't a brighter, keener or more popular newspaper man in the state, and his training and experience render him amply qualified to fill any position. He is thoroughly Democratic, and comes from good old New Hampshire Jeffersonian Democratic stock, being a nephew of the late U. S. Senator Moses Norris. He is a member of Storer Post No. 1, G. A. R., a Mason and Odd Fellow, Redman and Elk.

District No. 2.—JOHN C. RAY, Manchester. Republican, Superintendent of the State Industrial school, married; age, 66. Born in Hopkinton and has resided in Dunbarton and Chicopee, Mass., served as selectman and superintendent of schools and has been a justice of the peace 40 years. When he was a member of the House in 1852 he was, with one exception, the youngest member of the house, but his youth did not prevent him from becoming one of the most active and influential members. Dunbarton honored him subsequently by electing him chairman of the board of selectmen and superintendent of schools, positions which he filled to the satisfaction of all. July 2, 1874, he became superintendent of the State Industrial School and has filled the position so acceptably that he has been year by year unanimously re-elected, notwithstanding his often repeated desire to retire from the position. Mr. Ray's administration of affairs there has been characterized by great kindness but unflinching firmness in his dealing with the wayward youth intrusted to him, and it would be hard to find a man who could manage the farm more successfully. Under his faithful management the institution has taken rank in the forefront of similar institutions in this country. He was one of the trustees of the normal school and has always taken a deep interest in educational affairs. He also takes great interest in stock-raising and owns one of the best stock farms in Dunbarton or even Merrimack county. Member of the House in 1852, 53, 54 and 81.

District No. 3.—EDWARD O. BLUNT, Nashua. Republican, Congregationalist, merchant, married; age, 46. Born in Nashua, educated there and always resided there. Has held a number of city offices and represented his ward in the board of Aldermen for three years, only one other person having that record in the ward. Is very prominent in city politics and was chairman of the City Committee in 1888 and 1892; one of the board of Police Commissioners for Nashua, which office he resigned upon being elected Councilor. Is a Knight Templar and 32d Mason, also one of the Directors and Treasurer of the Masonic building association; trustee of City Savings Bank and Security Trust Co., a Knight of Pythias, member New Hampshire club and the Congregational club. Served in the House in 1881 and in the Senate in 1887. Always a Republican.

District No. 4.—FRANK N. PARSONS, Franklin. Republican, no religious preference stated, lawyer, married; age, 38. Born in Dover, Sept. 3, 1854. Educated at Dartmouth College. Has served as State Reporter since June, 1891. Member of the Constitutional Convention of 1889. Always a Republican.

District No. 5.—HERBERT B. MOULTON, Lisbon. Democrat, engaged in the lumber and live stock business, doing an extensive business as drover,

married; age, 46. Born in Lyman July 5, 1846. Educated in the common schools. Is a man of sound judgment and served the town of Lyman as member of the House in 1876 and 77 and was member from Lisbon in 1885. Is an active Democrat.

SENATE.

The senate is composed of 24 members. Fifteen are Republicans and nine are Democrats.

The oldest member is Hon. Newton S. Huntington of Hanover, who is 72, and the youngest is Hon. George F. Hammond of Nashua, who is 32. Two of the members are between 30 and 40 years of age, eleven between 40 and 50, five between 50 and 60, three between 60 and 70 and three between 70 and 80. All are natives of the State except four, one having been born in Maine, one in Massachusetts, one in Ohio and one in Scotland. Five were born in the towns where they now reside. Three are college graduates and seven received an academic education. Seventeen have been members of the House, one in both the House and senate, two of the House and Constitutional Convention of 1889, and one of that convention.

In religious belief six are Congregationalists, two Catholics, two Universalists, one Episcopalian, one Baptist and one Unitarian.

Three of the members are single and one of these is a widower.

The profession or occupation of the Senators is as follows: Farmers, 4; merchants, 3; lawyers, 3; manufacturers, 2, and one each bank president, mill superintendent, grocer, salesman, formerly a druggist, dealer in live stock and butcher, farmer and merchant, lumber dealer, manufacturer and merchant, engaged in settling estates, etc., publisher, and undertaker.

District No. 1.—PEARSON G. EVANS, Gorham. Democrat.

District No. 2.—EDWARD WOODS, Bath. Democrat, lawyer, president of savings bank and officer in several lumber companies, married; age, 57. Born in Bath Oct. 24, 1835 and has resided

there except three years in Littleton. Educated at Phillips Exeter Academy and Dartmouth College. Has served as county solicitor and as town treasurer for 20 years, also on school committee and was aide-de-camp on Gov. Weston's staff. Member of the House in 1873 and 74. Always a Democrat.

District No. 3.—NEWTON S. HUNTINGTON, Hanover. Republican, Baptist, bank president, married; age, 72. Born in Lebanon. Is the son of Elias and Lucinda (Putnam) Huntington. He was educated at the public schools of Hanover and at New London academy. His father, who was a farmer, died in Mr. Huntington's infancy, when the family moved to Hanover. Until 33 years of age Mr. Huntington remained on a farm, when he went into trade, continuing about seven years. In 1865 he organized the Dartmouth National bank, of which he was chosen cashier, and was elected treasurer of the Dartmouth Savings bank, and held these positions fourteen years, when he was chosen president of both banks, and holds both offices at present. In 1879 he went abroad; traveled through Scotland, England, France, Germany, Italy, and Switzerland, remaining away from home three months. He has travelled extensively through the United States and Canada, visiting every state east of the Rocky Mountains. He married, April 30, 1843. Mary, daughter of Deacon Isaac and Lucy (Chandler) Bridgman, of Hanover, and has two daughters, Ellen M., who married Prof. Robert Fletcher of the Thayer Department of Dartmouth College and Fanny C., who married Prof. Charles P. Chase, now treasurer of the two banks and treasurer of Dartmouth College, and has filled every office in the gift of the town. Moderator over thirty times; member of the House in 1858, 1859, 1885, 1887, 1889 and 1891. Dartmouth College bestowed the degree of A. M. in 1887.

District No. 4.—CHARLES H. DAMON, Campton. Baptist, grocery salesman, married; age, 41. Born in Lowell, Sept. 16, 1851. Educated in the Campton common schools. Was a member of the Constitutional convention of 1889, and of the House in 1891.

District No. 5.—FRANK K. HOBBS, Ossipee. Democrat, farmer, married, age, 51. Born in Tamworth Nov. 4, 1841. Educated at Wolfeboro and N. E. Masonic Institute, Effingham. Served in Co. F, 18th N. H. Vols., and discharged as orderly sergeant. Has held all the various town offices and was a member of the House in 1875, 77, 78, 81 and 85. Always an active Democrat.

District No. 6.—GEORGE A. HATCH, Laconia. Democrat, no religious preference, formerly a druggist, married; age, 44. Born in Meredith and has resided in New York city and Boston. Educated at New Hampton. Educated himself and never had a dollar that he did not earn by his own exertion. Has always taken an active interest in the politics of the town and is at present chairman of the town committee. Served as town clerk in 1876 and 77. Member of the House in 1878. Always a Democrat.

District No. 7.—SHEPARD L. BOWERS, Newport. Republican, lawyer, married; age, 65. Born in Acworth Dec. 13, 1827. Worked on his father's farm until 21 years old, when he began a course of study; fitted for college at Kimball Union Academy and at Thetford Vt., Academy; engaged in teaching several terms at Leominister and Fitchburg, Mass., and also was principal of the High schools in Acworth and South Acworth. Entered Dartmouth College in 1852, after which he read law with Hon. Asa Fowler of Concord, and was admitted to the bar in 1856 and began practice at Newport, where he has been actively engaged in his profession ever since. Was married in 1859 to Thankful M. Newell of Newport, who died in 1861. Nine years later was married to Susan E. Cofran of Goshen, served as Register of Probate 20 years and solicitor 4 years. Delegate to the Republican National conventions, at Baltimore in 1864 and afterwards at the convention in Chicago in 1884. He takes a lively interest in the growth and welfare of his town and was director of the Newport Savings bank at the time of its incorporation; is now president of the Newport Improvement Company. Aside from his active business life he is an extensive reader of literature and has written and delivered many essays and lectures. His children are John A.,

born March 2, 1872, and now a junior in Dartmouth college. Harry Natt, born September 21, 1876, and Mary Gertrude, born November 26, 1883. Member of the House in 1866, 85 and 86, and took a prominent and leading part, being an able, fluent, and brilliant debater.

District No. 8.—GEORGE S. PEAVEY, Greenfield. Democrat, Congregationalist, butcher and dealer in live stock, in which he does an extensive business as member of the firm of C. F. and G. S. Peavey; is also largely interested in real estate, principally pasturing, and handles thousands of cattle and sheep during the season; married; age, 57. Born in Greenfield, Feb. 14, 1835. Educated there, in Washington, Hopkinton, Pittsfield and Hancock. Has held the various town offices and himself and brother were directors of the First National Bank of Francestown and owned a tenth part of its stock when they voted to close it up in 1891. Member of the House in 1867 and 68. Always a Democrat.

District No. 9.—GEORGE C. PRESTON, Henniker. Republican, Congregationalist, merchant, married; age, 44. Born in Manchester. Educated at Francestown Academy. Has lived in Henniker over twenty years and been in the same business all of the time under different styles, at present associated with his brother under the style of Preston Bros., doing a general business, not being strictly confined to store trade, but do something in several lines, including some real estate and quite a fruit business, handling nearly all the fruit produced in the town. Is a Mason, Odd Fellow, and Granger, being a firm believer in any society that has for its object the good of humanity. Served as postmaster 4 years and town clerk 6. Member of the House in 1891. Always a Republican.

District No. 10.—JOSEPH B. WALKER, Concord. Republican, married, farmer; age, 70. Born in Concord, June 12, 1822. Graduated from Yale College in 1844 and afterwards at the Harvard law school, and admitted to the N. H. bar in 1847. Left the profession to care for inherited estates, a large farm and general business. Is an officer in many financial companies and state boards. Has contributed much to historic research and the agricultural interests of the state. Member of the House in 1866 and 67.

District No. 11.—JOHN WHITAKER, Penacook. Democrat, married; age, 56. Born in Hopkinton, but has lived in Ward One, since 1852. He comes of the best old New England stock, his father being a soldier in the war of 1812, and his grandfather fought at Bunker Hill, and served later in the ranks of the Continental army. Mr. Whitaker had traveled over sixteen of the states and territories before coming of age, and wisely concluding that the state of his birth was the best place for him, he settled in Fisherville, now Penacook, in the year before mentioned, entering the service of his brother-in-law, Seth B. Hoyt, who was engaged in the livery business. Here he was quite a knight of the whip for several years, and finally went into the same business on his own account and continued it until 1866, when in company with the firm of Caldwell and Amsden, he engaged in the manufacture of lumber at the borough, at the privilege now occupied in part by the new Holden Woolen Company and Electrical Machine Works. Here he transacted a lucrative business, up to 1891, when he sold the privilege to Hon. Charles H. Amsden. He has ever been one of the most active, as well as one of the most popular residents of Penacook, taking an active part in all that concerned the welfare of the village, or the interests of the people. Although a Democrat politically, in a strong Republican community, he has been chosen as assessor, in both branches of the city government, and in the state legislature. In the general overturn at the last election in Ward One, his vote was equal to the average given for the candidates elected on the Republican ticket, proving that his popularity is as lasting as it is deserving. He was married in 1859 to Miss Francis E. Caldwell, oldest daughter of the late B. F. Caldwell, and their home on Washington street is one of the pleasantest as it is one of the happiest in Penacook. He was appointed one of the Board of Water Commissioners last year. With the knowledge acquired from a practical business career, as well as being thoroughly informed in state and municipal affairs, none of the senators-elect will be better qualified for the honorable position.

District No. 12.—WILLIAM E. WATERHOUSE, Barrington. Republican, Universalist, but attends Congregational church, farmer and dealer in lumber, wood, flour, grain and groceries, married; age, 47. Born in Barrington, Jan. 31, 1845, and always resided there. Educated in the common and High school and at Franklin Academy, Dover. Served as town clerk 4 years, selectman six, county commissioner two, and moderator since 1886. Member of the Republican State Committee 18 years. Director of Concord and Rochester railroad and president and director of the Barrington Creamery Association. Member of the House in 1871 and 72 and member of Constitutional Convention of 1889. Republican always.

District No. 13.—CLEMENT J. WOODWARD, Keene. Republican, attends Episcopal church, publisher, married; age, 42. Born in Roxbury, Sept. 7, 1850. Educated at the Keene high school and Colby Academy. Is treasurer and manager of the Sentinel Printing Company, publishers of the daily Keene Evening Sentinel, and weekly New Hampshire Sentinel; director of the Keene National Bank, and has been a member of the Keene city government. Member of the Republican State Committee for many years, and always takes a lively interest in political affairs. Member of the House in 1887 and served on important committees. Always a Republican.

District No. 14.—WALTER L. GOODNOW, Jaffrey. Republican, Baptist, merchant, married; age, 41. Born in Winchendon, Mass., and has resided in Lyme, and Fitzwilliam Educated in the public schools. Member of the House in 1889. Always a Republican.

District No. 15.—JOHN McLANE, Milford, attends the Congregational church, manufacturer of post-office equipments, married; age, 41. Born in Scotland in 1852, and came to this country with his parents when two years of age. Member of the House in 1885-86, 1887-'8, and of the senate in 1891, and was chosen president of the senate and made an admirable presiding officer. Was always a Republican.

District No. 16.—FREEMAN HIGGINS, Manchester. Republican, first and last, Supt. of Amoskeag Company's machine shop, Congregationalist, married; age, 62. Born in Standish,

Me., resided in Lowell, Lawrence and Boston, but for the last 30 years in Manchester. Educated in the Lowell public schools and at Standish Academy.

District No. 17.—ALFRED G. FAIR-BANKS, Manchester. Republican, Congregationalist, undertaker, widower; age, 70. Born in Francestown and educated in the common schools and academy in that town. Served as deputy sheriff and jailor from 1865 to 1874; county commissioner, 1883 to 89. Member of the House in 1881. Formerly a Whig.

District No. 18.—LEONARD P. REYNOLDS, Manchester. Democrat, Catholic, wholesale and retail dealer in tobacco, cigars and smokers' articles, single; age, 40. Born in New Boston, Sept. 12, 1852, and received his education there and in Manchester. Is a public-spirited citizen; served in the city council in 1879 and 80, and as alderman in 1883, 84, 85, 86, 87 and 88.

District No. 19.—JOSEPH W. HOWARD, Nashua. Republican, Universalist, furniture manufacturer and merchant, married; age, 48. Born in Washington, Nov. 22, 1844. Educated at New London. Served as selectman, councilman and alderman and on the board of education 12 years. Member of the House in 1887. Always a Republican.

District No. 20.—GEORGE F. HAMMOND, Nashua. Republican, Protestant, lumber dealer, single; age, 34. Born in Nashua, June 8, 1854. Has served as a selectman and was a member of the House in 1891.

District No. 21.—JOHN D. LYMAN, Exeter. Republican. Liberal Congregationalist, engaged in settling estates, etc., married; age, 69. Born in Milton, July 3, 1833; resided there till 1855, in Farmington till 1869, and since then in Exeter. Liberally educated in Milton, Parsonsfield, Me., Rochester, and Gilmanton. He has addressed agricultural fairs, farmers' meetings, and various other meetings in this state, Massachusetts, Rhode Island, New York City, New Jersey, Wisconsin, and Canada. Served as bank commissioner and has been much interested in agriculture and forestry; served as school committee in three towns; visitor to West Point Military Academy, 1865; trustee of Normal School, Agricultural College, and N. H. Orphans' Home; lecturer of State Grange fifteen years; president of State Temperance Society; also bank cashier; bank commissioner; member of board of agriculture; member of the House six years, and of the Senate two years; delegate to Constitutional Convention of 1889; delegate to Boston and Atlanta, Ga., American Forestry Commission; and secretary of state three years. Was formerly a Free-Soil Whig. Is a popular citizen and was elected senator by a handsome majority.

District No. 22.—JOHN C. TASKER, Dover. Republican, Congregationalist, grocer, married; age, 49. Born in Rochester and has resided in Dover thirty years and always in the state. Educated at Rochester. Served as selectman, and treasurer of Odd Fellows. Member of the House in 1881 and 83. Always a Republican.

District No. 23.—ANDREW KILLOREN, Dover. Democrat, Catholic, clothier, single; age, 38. Born in Cincinnati and educated in the public schools. Served as assessor in 1882 and 83 and a member of the House in 1887, 89 and 91, and proved a popular and valuable member.

District No. 24.—CALVIN PAGE, Portsmouth. Democrat, Unitarian, lawyer, married; age, 46. Born in North Hampton, and has resided in Portsmouth since 1865, where he stands in the front rank of his profession. Educated in the common schools and at Phillips Exeter Academy. Has served as mayor, judge of police court, city solicitor; was U. S. Collector of Internal Revenue from 1885 to 1889. Is city water commissioner and member of board of education and high school committee now and for many years past. Member of the Constitutional Convention of 1889. Always a Democrat and is one of the trusted leaders of his party.

HOUSE.

The House is composed of 358 members. Of these 210 are Republicans and 148 are Democrats.

The oldest member is Gilman Corning of Salem, who is 77. The youngest member is John J. Lynch of Ward 5, Manchester, who is but 22, having been born in that city Nov. 19, 1870.

Ten of the members are between 20 and 30 years of age, 95 between 30 and 40, 127 between 40 and 50, 68 between 50 and 60, 45 between 60 and 70, and 3 who have passed the limit of threescore and ten. All but 81 were born in the state, 20 were born in Vermont, 19 in Massachusetts, 17 in Maine, 9 in the province of Quebec, 3 in Rhode Island, 2 in Ireland, 2 in England, 2 in New York, and one each, in Norway and Cape Breton, and 105 were born in the towns which they represent.

Twelve received a collegiate education, and the remainder were educated in the public schools and academies.

There are 41 unmarried members and 9 of them are widowers.

In religious belief or preference there are 61 Congregationalists, 35 Methodists, 31 Universalists, 24 Catholics, 19 Baptists, 17 Unitarians, 11 Free Baptists, 10 Episcopalians, 5 Adventists, 5 Liberals, 3 Christians, 3 Presbyterians, one each Atheist, Friend, and Lutheran; one who believes in truth and honesty; one who takes the broad ground of liberality to all; one who believes in Christianity but belongs to no sect, one who believes in the Bible without any twisting, one who believes in that which will do the most good to the largest number, and one whose motto is "Be good and do good."

Thirty-six have served in the House before, one in the House and Senate, 4 in the Constitutional Convention of 1889, 3 in the House and the Constitutional Convention of 1889, one in the House and in three Constitutional Conventions, one in the House and the Constitutional Convention of 1876, one in the House, Senate and last two Constitutional Conventions, one in the Senate, one in the Constitutional Convention of 1876, and one who was a member of the Massachusetts legislature while living in that State.

By profession or occupation there are 83 farmers, besides one each who combine that occupation with that of the produce shipping business, saw mill proprietor, jobber, lumber dealer, merchant, mica-miner, and wood dealer, four with that of blacksmith, three with that of lumberman, three with that of hotel keeper and two with that of carpenter, making over 100 members of the House who are engaged in tilling the soil.

There are 31 merchants, 19 manufacturers, 15 lawyers, 6 physicians, 6 superintendents, 5 mechanics, 3 machinists, 3 loom-fixers, 3 retired from business, 3 blacksmiths, 3 overseers, 3 hotel keepers, 3 carpenters and builders, 3 railroad station agents, 2 book-keepers, 2 druggists, 2 grocers, 2 lumbermen, 2 painters, 2 shoe cutters, and one each agent, apothecary, assistant station agent and telegraph operator, auctioneer and real estate broker, banker, butcher, carpenter, cigar maker, clerk of supreme court, commercial traveller, concrete paver, contractor and teamster, cooper, editor, editor and publisher, engineer, expressman, foreman, forger, general business, hair dresser, harness maker, horse shoer, insurance agent, jeweler, law student, liveryman, live stock dealer, marble and granite dealer, mason, merchant tailor, merchant and lumberman, merchant, farmer and saw mill proprietor, merchant and manufacturer, plumber and steam fitter, postmaster, probate business and insurance, railroad conductor, railroad passenger agent, railroad road master, roofing business, surveyor, teamster, and telegraph operator.

A

ABBOT, FRANCIS L., Concord, Ward 6. Democrat. Episcopal, secretary of the Abbot-Downing Company, which has a world-wide reputation, single; age, 49. Born in Concord, May 20, 1843, and always made the capital city his home. Educated at St. Paul's school. Is a public-spirited, popular citizen. Never held political office and always voted the Democratic ticket.

ADAMS, IRA H., Derry. Republican, Methodist, physician, married; age, 46. Born in Pomfret, Vt., Aug. 10, 1846, and resided in Hooksett from 1874 to 1882 and since then in Derry. Educated at the Vt. State Normal school, Kimball Union Academy, and Dartmouth Medical College. Has served as a member of the school board.

ALDRICH, LEWIS W., Westmore-land. Republican, Baptist, farmer, married; age, 50. Born in Westmoreland and has lived in Providence, Fitchburg and Worcester. Served in the 9th N. H. Vols., enlisting Aug. 17, 1862; was wounded at South Mountain Sept. 14, 1862, and rejoined his regiment after the battle of Fredericksburg, Dec. 10, 1862, and served until the close of the war. Been supervisor of the check-list.

ALLEN, FREDERICK, Manchester, Ward 4. Republican, Congregationalist, dealer in harnesses, carriages, etc., married; age, 58. Born in Northampton, Mass., April 20, 1834, and came to Manchester in 1850. Served as superintendent of the city farm from 1876 to 1883. Always a Republican.

ALLEN, WILLIAM J., Manchester, Ward 5. Democrat, Catholic, loom-fixer, married; age, 25. Born at Gravesend, Eng., and came to this country when one year old. Educated at Park street grammar school, Manchester. Commenced work in the Stark mills and has worked himself into his present position. Never ran for office before.

B

BADGER, FRANKLIN L., Concord, Ward 6. Democrat, in religious belief he takes the broad ground of liberality to all, foundry foreman, married; age, 35. Born in Benton, June 28, 1857 and lived for a time in Warren, where he was educated in the public schools and at Haverhill academy. Always a Democrat.

BAILEY, CHARLES R., Londonderry. Republican, married; age, 41. Born at West Lebanon; resided in Scranton, Pa., until 1867, in Manchester until 1883 and in Londonderry since. Has served as selectman three years.

BAILEY, WILLIAM H., Raymond. Democrat, married; age, 50. Born in Littleton. At an early age his parents removed to Manchester, where he attended the public schools, and resided until 1868, when he went to Raymond and engaged in general merchandise business; after 24 years, sold out in January, 1891, and spent the following winter in California; has not engaged in business since. Was always a Democrat.

BAKER, ARTEMUS O, Wilton. Democrat, merchant.

BAKER, STILLMAN H., Hillsboro. Republican, no religious preference, auctioneer and real estate broker, firm of Manahan and Baker, married; age, 38. Born in Croydon and has resided in Concord; spent ten years in the West Indies and Central America. Served as selectman and tax collector. Always a Republican.

BARTLETT, GEORGE E., Unity. Democrat, farmer, married; age, 66. Born in Unity and has resided in Newport. Member of the House in 1879. Always a Democrat.

BATCHELDER, ALBERT, North Hampton. Republican.

BATCHELDER, NATHANIEL P., Ashland. Republican.

BEATTIE, ALEXANDER M., Lancaster. Republican.

BECKER, FORREST, Newcastle. Democrat, Methodist, shoe cutter, married; age, 32. Born in Kittery, Me., Nov. 13, 1860. Educated in Newcastle. Member of the Constitutional Convention of 1889. Always a Democrat.

BLAIS, EDMUND, Pittsburg. Democrat, Catholic, hotel keeper proprietor of the Pittsburg house, married. Born in Canada and has lived in Pittsburg the last 20 years. Educated at Montreal and other Canadian schools. Has served as moderator, supervisor, etc. For the special session of 1890 he was elected to fill out the unexpired term of representative Bean of Pittsburg.

BLANDIN, AMOS N., Bath. Democrat.

BLOOD, HORATIO C., Wentworth. Democrat, Universalist preference, carpenter and builder, married; age, 54. Born in Wentworth, Aug. 5, 1838, and has always lived there, excepting two years. Served as selectman 4 years. Always a Democrat.

BOWEN, EDWIN N., Fitzwilliam. Republican, Universalist, manufacturer of chairs, married; age, 40. Born in Richmond, Nov. 14, 1843. Enlisted Aug.

12, 1861, as a private in the 3d N. H. Vols., discharged Aug. 3, 1865, as 1st. Lieut. in command of Co. B. Was in all the great battles that the 3d. was engaged in. After the war engaged in the lumber business in Richmond from 1866 to 1882, and since then has carried on his present business in Fitzwilliam. Served as selectman 8 years, also as justice of the peace and deputy sheriff. Member of the House in 1875 and 76.

BOWEN, JOHN, Walpole. Democrat.

BRIGHAM, GEORGE H., Nashua, Ward 1. Republican, been in the grocery business for 22 years, married; age, 42. Born in Nashua, educated there and always resided there. Represented his ward two years in the city council and as alderman in 1892.

BRIGHAM, HOSEA W., Winchester. Republican, Universalist, lawyer, married; age, 55. Born at Whitingham, Vt., May 30, 1837, and educated there and at Barre Academy. Served on the school board and was member of the Constitutional Convention of 1889.

BRONSON, MYRON S., Landaff. Democrat, believes in truth and honesty, farmer, married; age, 51. Born in Landaff, Jan. 20, 1841, and always resided there. Has served as supervisor six years. Member of the House in 1887. Always a Democrat.

BROOKS, WINSUR A., Franconia. Democrat, lumberman, married; age, 31. Born in Landaff, Jan. 3, 1861. Served as selectman 2 years.

BROOKS, ZENOPHON W., Hancock. Democrat, farmer, single; age, 55. Born in Hancock, Nov. 16, 1837. Educated there and always resided there. Has served on the school committee and as selectman.

BROWN, CHARLES R., Deerfield. Republican, insurance agent.

BROWN, EDMUND H., Concord, Ward 1. Republican, Baptist, superintendent of Concord Axle Co., which carries on a large and flourishing business, married; age, 35. Born in Penacook, Oct. 29, 1857. Educated at Penacook

Academy and the Massachusetts Institute of Technology. Is a popular citizen and has served six years on the State Committee of his party. Always a Republican.

BROWN, JOHN H., Merrimack. Republican.

BROWN, ROBINSON, Goffstown. Republican, Protestant, stationery engineer, married; age 64. Born in New Boston and educated in the Auburn and Nashua public schools. Followed the sea 8 years and at the age of 20 was second mate of the "Two Brothers." In 1851 went to California, and enlisted in 1861, and was discharged for disability in 1865. Served as town treasurer 17 years.

BRYANT, WYATT, Tamworth. Republican, attends Congregational church, mechanic, contractor and builder, and owns a good farm, married; age, 60 years. Born in Tamworth and lived in Moultonborough about 5 years. Always a strong Republican.

BRYSON, JOHN, Manchester, Ward 8. Democrat.

BUFFUM, JOHN A., Monroe. Republican, farmer, married; age, 55. Born in Monroe, May 6, 1837. Educated in Vermont. Has served as selectman and supervisor.

BULLARD, WILLIE E., Lancaster. Republican, Methodist, merchant of the firm of Frank Smith and Co., flour, grain, provisions and groceries, married; age, 37. Born in Lancaster, Dec. 7, 1855. Educated there and always resided there. Has served as selectman. Always a Republican.

BURNHAM, WILLIE G., Mont Vernon. Republican, proprietor of the "Grand" hotel; age, 42. Born in Lowell, Sept. 15, 1850, married the daughter of T. H. Richardson of Mont Vernon in 1875, and she died in 1887. Has served as selectman, and was elected representative by 26 majority.

BURROUGHS, JOHN H., Bow. Democrat, Episcopal, farmer, married; age, 47. Born in Londonderry, in June, 1845. Educated at Pittsfield Academy and Bryant and Stratton's Commercial College. Served as selectman 6 years, also as postmaster and on the board of education. Member White Mountain Lodge, I. O. O. F., Concord.

BURTON, WILLIAM P., Lebanon. Republican, Congregationalist, engaged in probate business and insurance, married; age, 64. Born in Norwich, Vt., Dec. 2, 1828, and has resided in Maryland and Virginia. Educated at Kimball Union Academy, Thetford Academy, and Dartmouth College, class of '52. Was postmaster at West Lebanon from Jan. 1, 1867, to April 1, 1888, over twenty-one years. Member of the Constitutional Convention of 1889. Member of the House in 1891. Formerly a Whig.

C

CARROLL, EDWARD H., Warner, Republican, attends Baptist church, merchant, married; age, 38. Born in Sutton, Oct. 31, 1854, and resided there until 13 years old, since then in Warner. Was appointed postmaster in Oct., 1877, and held the office until July, 1884, when he resigned voluntarily, said to be the only postmaster in New Hampshire who resigned without request, or because of a belief in rotation of office. Was town treasurer in 1885 and 86, member of High School board from 1886 to 1889. Was elected treasurer of Merrimack county in 1890 in a Democratic county, which office expires in April, 1893, is a hustler in politics as well as in business. Entered into co-partnership in business with his father, A. C. Carroll, at the age of 18, and has continued at the same store and place as clerk and partner for 25 years; is one of the prominent business men of Merrimack county and enjoys the confidence of a large circle of friends, is generous, enterprising, frank, broad-minded and an honored citizen, a F. A. A. M., and has been treasurer of Harris Lodge for the past ten years, is a Trustee and incoporator of the Union Guaranty Savings Bank of Concord, and interested in many industries, and in everything labors for the welfare of the town, and is among the brightest and most intelligent of New Hampshire's sons. His influence will be felt in the legislature, and a bright future is undoubtedly before him.

CARTER, HENRY H., Gilsum. Republican, Universalist, farmer, married; age, 49. Born in Surry, March 1, 1843. He lived 20 years in Springfield and Weathersfield, Vt., 4 years in West Springfield, Mass., 11 years in Surry, and since then in Gilsum. Has served as supervisor and selectman. Always a Republican.

CARTER, NORRIS C., Swanzey. Republican, Baptist, farmer, married; age, 44. Born in Fitzwilliam. Has served as selectman 6 years.

CHAMBERLIN, ROBERT N., Berlin. Republican, Congregationalist, lawyer, married; age, 34. Born in New York. Has served on the board of education and as selectman. Member of the House in 1889 and took high rank as a debater. Always a Republican.

CHAPMAN, FRANK H., Franklin. Republican, Unitarian, druggist, married; age, 44. Born in Lowell. Lived there 3 years, 20 years in Lawrence, 3 in Brooklyn, and for the past 18 in Franklin. Educated in Lawrence. Has served as president of the N. H. Pharmacy Association. Was always a Republican.

CHASE, ALFRED G., Canterbury. Democrat, liberal in religious views, farmer, widower; age, 62. Born in Canterbury and has lived in Boston till within the last 10 years. Has served as selectman and was a member of the Constitutional Convention of 1889.

CHASE, FRANKLIN N., Somersworth. Democrat, Universalist, single; age, 27. Born in Andover, Mass., Nov. 16, 1865, and educated there. Served as Boston and Maine ticket agent at Great Falls station and was promoted July 1, 1891, to be N. E. Passenger Agent of the same road, and Aug. 1, 1892, was again promoted to be Assistant General Passenger and Ticket Agent, in all of which positions he proved to be an active, energetic, and very popular official of the company. He is a thoroughgoing Democrat, and has been one of the trusted leaders of his party in the sharp contests that have in late years occurred in Somersworth. He served efficiently as town treasurer in 1889 and 1890, and was a member of the House in 1891.

CHENEY, HARRY M., Lebanon. Re-

publican, Unitarian, editor of the Free Press, and insurance agent, single; age, 32. Born in Newport, March 8, 1860, and has lived in Lebanon since 1861. Educated at Colby Academy, class of '82, and Bates College, class of '86. Has served as auditor of state printer's accounts and was always a Republican.

CHICKERING, JACOB E., Pembroke. Republican, Methodist, jeweler, single; age, 18. Born in Suncook, Aug. 30, 1833, and always resided there. Educated at Pembroke Academy. Has served as selectman and town treasurer.

CLARK, BENJAMIN FRANKLIN. Conway. Republican, Unitarian, mill superintendent, married; age, 49. Born in Townsend, Mass., June 25, 1843, and has lived in Lowell, Fitchburg and Boston. He enlisted in 1861, in the 15th Mass. Vols., commanded by Gen. Charles Devens, and served in Co B. during all the battles in which the regiment was engaged, until the battle of Antietam, where he was severely wounded in the head, causing the total loss of the right eye, and was honorably discharged from the service. He has taken an active part in Grand Army matters; is trustee and president of the Conway Savings bank, and was a member of the House in 1891.

CLARK, CHARLES C., Manchester, Ward 4. Republican, Protestant, fancy goods dealer, married; age, 32. Born in Chester, June 5, 1860, and has lived in Manchester since 1875.

CLARK, GEORGE M., Manchester, Ward 3. Republican, Protestant, millinery and fancy goods dealer, married; age, 35. Born in Chester, July 24, 1857, and has lived in Manchester since 1884. Served on the school committee in Chester and in the common council in Manchester.

CLARK, JOHN H., Acworth. Republican, believes in Christianity, farmer, married; age, 62. Born in Newbury, March 5, 1830, and has lived in Acworth since 1858. Educated at New London. Served as selectman 5 years, supervisor 2. Formerly a Whig.

CLEASBY, GEORGE B., Hollis. Democrat, country store keeper, married; age, 48. Born in Warren in 1844, and has resided in Wentworth and Plymouth.

CLOW, STEPHEN W., Wolfeborough. Republican, Adventist, carpenter and farmer; married; age, 37. Born in Wolfeborough, April 2, 1855. Was brought up on a farm and followed that business until about his eighteenth year; attended the Wolfeborough and Tuftonborough Academy a part of the time the following four years, teaching common schools through the winter and for several years after. Is justice of the peace, and member of the Morning Star Lodge No. 61, A. F. and A. M., of Wolfeborough. Is serving his 7th consecutive year as selectman and 5th as chairman.

COFFIN, HENRY P., Newport. Republican.

COLBY, GEORGE H., Plymouth. Democrat, Universalist, Railroad station agent, married; age, 51. Born in Pembroke, April 15, 1841, and has resided in Manchester and Bethlehem. Educated in the Manchester public schools, graduating from the High in April, 1859. Has served as supervisor and moderator. Member of the House in 1891 and was active in its proceedings. Born a Democrat.

COLBY, MOSES N., Manchester, Ward 7. Republican, Universalist, overseer of pipe fitting for Amoskeag M'f'g. Co., with which he has been connected for over 26 years. Born in Dunbarton, April 18, 1845 and has lived in Manchester since 1865. Always a Republican.

COLE, GEORGE H., Grafton. Democrat, Christian, farmer, married; age, 42. Born in Grafton, Dec. 7, 1850, educated there and always resided there. Served as selectman 3 years. Always a Democrat.

COLE, GUY, Columbia. Republican, farmer, married; age, 32. Born in Columbia, and was an only child. His father died when he was 13 years old, leaving himself and mother with almost nothing, but by hard work and trying to be honest he has a comfortable home, and all the friends a man need to have. Has never held any office before.

COLE, WALLACE W., Salem. Republican, attends Methodist church, butcher, married; age, 37. Born in Boxford, Mass., Nov. 19, 1855, and has lived in Amesbury and Andover, Mass. Served as selectman 3 years. Always a Republican.

COLLINS, ALBERT, Grantham. Republican, manufacturer and dealer in shingles, married; age, 62. Born in Enfield, Sept. 16, 1837. Has lived in California and Lebanon.

COLONY, JOHN J., Keene, Ward 5. Democrat, Unitarian, woolen manufacturer, single; age, 28. Born in Keene, Nov. 14, 1864. Educated in the Keene High School and Harvard University, class of '85, and spent a year in the Harvard law school. Is 1st Lieut. Co. G. 2d Regt. N. H. N. G., and was a member of the city council in 1892.

CONNOR, WILLIAM H., South Newmarket. Republican. Has served as selectman.

COOK, GEORGE P., Rumney. Republican, Congregationalist, farmer, married; age, 47. Born in Rumney. Lived in Plymouth from 1870 to 1888 and served as selectman there. Member of the House in 1891.

COOPER, ARTHUR F., Exeter. Republican.

COPITHORN, RICHARD H., Campton. Republican, Episcopal, farmer, married; age, 41. Born in Boston, March 5, 1851; lived there 12 years, in Charlestown 13, and for the past 12 in Campton. Educated in the Boston and Charlestown public schools.

COPP, GEORGE W., Tuftonborough. Democrat, farmer; age, 38. Born Nov. 3, 1854. Has served as collector of taxes, selectman and town treasurer.

CORNING, GILMAN, Salem. Republican, Baptist, retired shoe manufacturer, widower; age, 77. Born in Londonderry, and lived in Haverhill, Mass., from 1836 to 1880, and was a member of the Massachusetts legislature in 1861 and 62. Was formerly a Whig and then Abolitionist. Voted for General Harrison in 1840, and his grandson in 1888 and 1892, and is probably the only member of the legislature who can make the same boast.

COURSER, THOMAS J., Webster. Democrat, farmer, married; age, 55. Born in Wilmot, July 20, 1837. Lived in Warner till 21 years of age, and then in Sutton for 8 years with Dr. Robert Lane, and for the past 26 years in Webster. Educated in the district and high schools in Warner and at Contoocook Academy. Served as county commissioner from 1887 to 1891. Is a progressive, popular citizen, and was always a Democrat, and elected from a Republican town.

CRAWFORD, ERASTUS A., Dover, Ward 2. Republican, Methodist, Insurance agent, senior member of the firm Crawford, Tolles and Co., married; age, 68. Born in Norfolk, N. Y., March 28, 1824. Lived at the White Mountains till 20 years of age and then for 40 years at Great Falls, and in Dover for the past 8 years. Educated in Bartlett, and at Rochester Academy. Is a son of Erastus Crawford and grandson of "Old Abel Crawford," of White Mountain fame, who was a member of the N. H. legislature in the 82d and 83d years of his age. Upon arriving at lawful age to vote, he became affiliated with the old Whig party and continued as such to its demise; was in at the birth of the Republican party and has been loyal to its principles ever since. In 1888 was elected as lay delegate to the Methodist General Conference at New York; in 1889 was elected by the N. H. Sunday School Association as delegate to the World's Sunday School Convention held in London; in 1891 was elected member of the common council from Ward 2, Dover.

CUMMINGS, CHARLES E., Nashua, Ward 1. Republican, attends Methodist church, but has liberal religious views, marble and granite dealer, married; age, 49. Born in Sutton, Aug. 5, 1843, and has lived in Concord and Manchester. Educated in the district school and at Colby Academy. Was selectman in Ward 6, Concord, 4 years, doorkeeper of the House in 1875 and 76, also of the Constitutional Convention of 1876, sergeant-at-arms of the House in 1877 and 78. Removed to Nashua in 1878; was a member of the city council in 1883 and 84, president of council the latter year, member of board of aldermen in 1891. Cast his first vote in 1864 for Lincoln.

CURRIER, OREN N., Eaton. Democrat, Baptist, farmer, married; age, 24. Born in Eaton and always resided there.

D

DALEY, PATRICK, Manchester, Ward 5. Democrat, Catholic, cooper, married; age, 27. Born in Manchester, Jan. 14, 1865. Educated at the Park street grammar school and Bryant and Stratton's College. Served as inspector of checklist and ward clerk. Always a Democrat.

DANFORTH, Edgar L., Lyndeboro. Republican.

DAVENPORT, SYLVESTER O., Hinsdale. Republican, Methodist, farmer and blacksmith, married; age, 63. Born in Hinsdale and always resided there. Educated there and at Brattleboro, Vt. Served at selectman 2 years.

DAVIS, JAMES, Alstead. Republican, farmer and mica miner, married; age, 42. Born in Springfield, Vt., Feb. 28, 1850, and has lived in Boston and Chicago. Educated in Springfield and in Woodstock, Vt., and the Roxbury, Mass., High school. Has served as supervisor and selectman. Was census enumerator in 1890, and is master of Ashuelot grange. Born a Republican, always straight, and hopes to die one.

DAVIS, LYMAN, Sullivan. Republican, Congregationalist, blacksmith, married; age, 47. Born in Stoddard, Sept. 25, 1845, and lived there till 1868 and since then in Sullivan. Educated in the district school and at Marlow Academy. Served as selectman 6 years, supervisor 3 years, and tax collector 2 years.

DAY, EDWARD O., Cornish. Republican, no religious preference, farmer, married; age, 54. Born in Cornish, June 21, 1838, and has always lived there excepting 8 years in Iowa. Has served as selectman 8 years, being chairman 3 years. Always a Republican.

DAY, FRED N., Stratford. Democrat, Liberal, lumberman, married; age, 45. Born in Northumberland, Aug. 25, 1847. Educated in the common school, at Lancaster Academy and State Normal School. Has served as selectman, treasurer, on the school committee, and delegate to the Constitutional Convention of 1889. Member of the House in 1874.

DEAN, HARRY G., Danbury. Democrat, believes in Christianity, but belongs to no sect, farmer, single; born in Danbury, Feb. 4, 1867, and always resided there. Educated at Proctor Academy, Andover. Served as selectman 4 years, two years as chairman. Always a Democrat.

DEMERITT, JOHN L., Effingham. Republican every time, trader and farmer and conducts a saw mill, married; age, 52. Born in Effingham and always resided there. Has served as highway surveyor and hog reeve, very important offices when well filled. He never thought he would like to attend his own funeral or write his own epitaph, and so leaves it for future historians to do, although he concludes they won't know half so much about him as he knows himself.

DERBY, JOHN H., Lyme. Republican.

DINSMORE, JOHN HOWARD, Windham. Republican, attends Presbyterian church, farmer, married; age, 52. Born in Windham, June 3, 1840, and always lived there. Served as selectman three terms and supervisor four. Always a straight Republican.

DODGE, JONATHAN T., Rochester, Ward 5. Democrat, hotel keeper, single; age, 49. Born in Rochester and always resided there. Educated in Boston and Andover, Mass. Has served as councilman.

DODGE, SMITH, Manchester, Ward 6. Republican, Methodist, wholesale produce dealer, married; age, 56. Born in Newbury, Vt., and has lived for the last 22 years in Manchester. Educated in the Vermont public schools. Always a Republican.

DODGE, WILLIAM F., Hopkinton. Republican, Congregationalist, farmer, married; age, 55. Born in Hopkinton and always resided there, excepting 5 years in Manchester. Served as selectman 5 years, being chairman three. Always a Republican.

DORT, EDWIN B., Troy. Republican, Congregationalist, connected with E. Buttrick and Co., wooden-ware manufacturers, single; age, 25. Born in Troy, Dec. 29, 1866. Educated at Cushing Academy, Ashburnham, Mass., and Eastman Business College, Poughkeepsie, N. Y. Is a member of Monadnock Lodge of Masons.

DOW, WILLIAM, Portsmouth, Ward 2. Democrat.

DOWNES, DANIEL, Andover. Democrat, Unitarian, merchant and lumberman, married; age, 54. Born in Salisbury, June 10, 1838. Educated in Lowell. Always a Democrat.

DOWNS, FRANK L., Manchester, Ward 3. Republican, Congregationalist, shoe dealer, married; age, 30. Born in Great Falls, Sept. 10, 1862, and educated in the Manchester public schools. Has been Captain of the Manchester Cadets since 1885, and is a Republican, now and forever.

DUNLAP, WILLIAM, Salisbury. Democrat, Baptist, merchant and farmer, married; age, 66. Born in Newburyport, Mass., Aug. 23, 1826, and has lived in Concord. Educated in Salisbury and Tilton. Has served as postmaster at West Salisbury for 36 years.

E

EASTMAN, CHARLES F., Littleton. Democrat, Congregationalist, engaged in general business, married; age, 51. Born in Littleton and always resided there. Educated in town schools and Thetford and West Randolph, Vt., and Kimball Union Academies, and Eastman's Business College, Poughkeepsie, N. Y. Served on board of education 11 years and treasurer of Union school district, 8 years, selectman 3 terms, chairman the last. Always a Democrat.

EASTMAN, SAMUEL C., Concord, Ward 4. Republican, no religious preference given, lawyer, married; age, 55. Born in Concord, and has always resided there. Educated at Brown University and Harvard Law School. Member of the House in 1883, and served as Speaker.

EATON, JOHN, Manchester, Ward 8. Democrat, Protestant, tobacco and cigar dealer, married; age, 50. Born in Corinth, Me., Aug. 17, 1842. Educated at Pittsfield, and resided for a time in Illinois, is a veteran of the war, a member of several societies, and an all-around good fellow, which goes far to account for his popularity as attested at the ballot-box. His war service was in two of New Hampshire's fighting regiments. In 1861 he enlisted in Company E, Second Regiment, and was with it two years, participating in the Peninsular campaign. In December, 1863, he became a member of Company H, Fourth Regiment, and served with that till the end of the war. At the battle of the "Mine" before Petersburg, Va., he was wounded badly and his deformed hand is a badge of good military service. Always a Democrat.

EATON, PERRY A., Weare. Democrat, Baptist, road master, married; age, 55. Born in Weare, May 27 1837, and educated there. Commenced railroad business as section hand at the age of 19, on the New Hampshire Central; after 4 years, was promoted to section foreman at North Weare; after 2 years, went to firing an engine from North Weare to Manchester, for 1 year; then accepted a position as division master on the Sullivan road; after 1 year, accepted an offer on the Vermont Valley railroad as division master; after a short time, went to work on the Cheshire railroad, as assistant road master, for 9 years, and then had an offer from the Concord railroad to go to work for them as assistant road master; after being assistant road master 4 years, was promoted to general road master, which position he still holds.

ELLINGWOOD, HIRAM E., Milan. Republican.

ELWELL, HENRY M., Langdon. Republican, Universalist, farmer, married; age, 53. Born in Langdon. April 13, 1830, and has always lived there. Educated at Chester and Tubbs Union Academies. Always a Republican.

EMERSON, JOHN D., Greenfield. Democrat, hotel and livery stable keeper.

EVERETT, EDWARD H., Nashua,

Ward 3. Democrat, Atheist, druggist, married; age, 37. Born in Henniker and resided for a time in Weare. Member of the House in 1885, and made a minority report as a member of the Committee on Education against the present town school law. Is an original thinker and a keen debater, with a large fund of humor to draw from. Always a Democrat of the Jeffersonian brand.

F

FARNUM, HENRY H., Concord, Ward 3. Republican, Congregationalist, contractor and teamster, married; age, 47. Born in West Concord. Educated at Boscawen, Meriden and Eastman Business College, Poughkeepsie, N. Y. Engaged in the grocery business 3 years with Capt. R. S. Davis, and in the meat and provision business 3 years, and was in business one year in Ohio. Served in the Heavy Artillery till the close of the war. Has been commander of Davis Post, G. A. R., and adjutant for the past 7 years. Is a Mason, and has served as ward clerk, selectman, and secretary of the Republican club for 8 years.

FARNUM, JOHN R., Marlboro. Republican, Protestant, farmer and blacksmith, married; age, 53. Born in Rhode Island, Jan. 18, 1839, and lived for a time in Fitchburg, Mass., and Dayton, O., and in Marlboro since 1881. Member of Fitchburg common council, selectman in Marlboro 3 years. Served 3 years in the 15th Mass. Vols. Taken prisoner at Gettysburg and escaped July 5. Always a Republican.

FAVOR, JOSEPH W., Hill. Republican, member of Christian church, married; age, 47. Born in Hill, Sept. 15, 1845. Educated in the common schools and at New Hampton. Served as tax collector 4 years, town clerk 2, selectman 4, and justice of the peace 5. Is a veteran of the 8th unattached Co. of Mass. Volunteers and a pensioner.

FAXON, CHARLES E., Nashua, Ward 3. Democrat.

FELLOWS, JOHN H., Brentwood. Republican, Baptist, box manufacturer, married; age, 42. Born in Brentwood, educated there and always resided there. Has served as selectman and was always a Republican.

FELLOWS, SMITH D., Bristol. Republican.

FELT, MARCELLUS H., Hillsborough. Republican, attends Methodist church, physician and surgeon, married; age, 47. Born in Sullivan, July 1, 1845, and has lived in Nelson, and Winchester, Davenport and Iowa City, Iowa, Boston, Chelsea and Templeton, Mass. Educated in the common and high schools, at the Maine Medical school and Dartmouth Medical College. Has served as moderator, trustee of public library 6 years, board of education 12 years, supervisor 2 years, town auditor 1 year, board of health 5 years. Has been active and prominent in the Masonic Institution, having held about all the offices in Lodge and Chapter, including that of D. D. Grand Master, 4th District N. H. Grand Lodge. Has also held several offices in the N. H. Medical Society, and been president of the N. H. Centre District Society.

FIELD, JOHN H., Nashua, Ward 8. Republican, Catholic, book-keeper, married; age, 34. Born in Manchester, Aug. 29, 1858. Served as alderman 2 years.

FERNALD, THOMAS E., Nottingham. Republican.

FLANDERS, CHARLES F., Wilmot. Democrat.

FLANDERS, GEORGE L., Littleton. Democrat.

FLETCHER, DANIEL A., Amherst. Republican, attends Congregational church, retired from business, single; age, 67. Born in Amherst, and has lived in Ogdensburg, N. Y., Toledo, O., Nashua, Iowa, and Memphis, Tenn., where he has engaged in business as a merchant, miller, and soapstone manufacturer. He has had an extensive business experience. Served as town clerk 5 years. Always a Republican.

FLETCHER, IRA E., Farmington. Democrat.

FLINT, WILLIAM WILLARD, Concord, Ward 7. Republican, Episcopal, married; age, 42. Born in Colebrook,

Aug. 16, 1850; is a son of the late Lyman T. Flint, formerly solicitor for Merrimack county and member of the legislature from the same ward. Educated in the Concord public schools, at Montpelier, Vt., at Dartmouth College, class of '71 and at Columbian Law School, Washington, in 1874. Afterwards practiced a short time in Clinton, Iowa. For several years past has been connected with St. Paul's School in a business and clerical capacity. Served as school committee for ten years and a trustee of the Concord public library.

FOLLANSBEE, PERLEY R., Dorchester. Democrat, Free Baptist, farmer, married; age, 57. Born in Danbury and has lived in Dorchester since 16 years of age. Has served as tax collector and selectman. Member of the House in 1891.

FOLLANSBY, WILLIAM H. C., Exeter. Republican.

FORD, ISAAC N., Groton. Republican, believes in the Bible as it is, without any twisting, engaged in the lumber business, married; age, 44. Born in Orange, July 10, 1848. Educated in the common school and at Canaan Union Academy. Has served as moderator, selectman and member of school board. Was a Democrat prior to 1876.

FOSKETT, LIBERTY W., Keene, Ward 2. Republican, Methodist, mechanic, married; age, 52. Born in Winchendon, Mass., Feb. 8, 1840, and has lived in Keene for 22 years. Served from Aug. 2, 1862, till the close of the war in the 36th Mass. Vols., and discharged as 2d Lieut. Is a G. A. R. member, and served two years as post commander and one year each as aide-de-camp, chief mustering officer and inspector, selectman 3 years, councilman and alderman 2 years each.

FOSTER, GEORGE J., Dover, Ward 1. Republican, Methodist, publisher of Foster's Daily and Weekly Democrat, married; age, 38. Born in Concord, in 1854, and has resided in Manchester and Portsmouth. Graduated at the high school in the latter city, class of '69. Has been a member of the school committee 7 years. Was an alternate to the Chicago Convention of 1884.

FOSTER, OLIVER H., Milford. Republican, Congregationalist, engaged in meat and provision business, married; age, 50. Born in Temple. Educated at Appleton Academy. Always a Republican.

FOWLER, WINTHROP, Pembroke. A life-long Democrat, farmer, married; age, 65. Born in Epsom, and has resided in Pembroke since 1845. Educated at Pembroke Academy and People's Literary Institute. Served as moderator 11 years, selectman 3, and auditor 8 years.

FRENCH, ALBERT S, Wilton. Democrat.

FROST, JOHN F., Manchester, Ward 7. Republican.

FRYE, CHARLES E., Laconia. Democrat.

FULLERTON, JOHN, Manchester, Ward 3. Republican, Congregationalist, superintendent of parks and commons for the past 4 years, married; age, 50. Born in Inverness, Province of Quebec. Came to Bradford at the age of 10, and in 1861 enlisted in the 4th N. H. Vols., and served till Aug. 23, 1865, and was mustered out as a Lieutenant. Always a straight Republican.

G

GALE, CYRUS E., Jackson. Democrat, Protestant, proprietor of Eagle Mountain House and engaged in farming, married; age, 43. Born in Groton, Vt., July 28, 1840, and has lived in Jackson since 1850. Served as selectman 6 years, on the school board, etc. Served as moderator for the past 15 years. Is a strong advocate for reform in the present system of working highway taxes, claiming that three-fourths of the time and money is wasted. He took the contract last spring to make the roads better in the town of Jackson for 15 years for 1-2 of what has been raised heretofore (or 25 cents a poll and 1-4 of one per cent on resident valuation) and gave $3,000 bonds for faithful performance of the same. He says every town should have one man within its limits who should "take the risk of building all its highways for 15 years, and give bonds for

the same, the roads subject to the approval of the selectmen, and the town to assume all damages by accident. The surveyor should receive a certain per cent on the valuation, so if there is an increase he will get it. Why 15 years? Because what extra he puts in a road will accrue to him at the latter end, and by so doing improve our roads quickly. If the town surveyor should lay out three times his percentage the first two or three years his money would come back three-fold. This is the only sure way to improve our highways of which there is great need.". Always a Democrat.

GALE, HIRAM C., Laconia. Democrat, farmer, married; age, 55. Born in Warren, June 12, 1837, and lived there until 1884. Has served as tax collector and supervisor. Always a Democrat.

GEORGE, ALBERT, Goffstown. Democrat.

GEORGE, FRANK H., Concord, Ward 4. Republican, Congregationalist, merchant, married; age, 52. Born in Plymouth, July 12, 1840, and has lived in Bristol and Laconia, but in Concord for the last 18 years. Is a veteran of the late war of the rebellion, serving in the department of the Gulf. Is now prominent in the Grand Army and has held several offices in E. E. Sturtevant Post 2, of Concord, and at present is serving his second term as quartermaster-general of the department of New Hampshire. Republican always.

GILBERT, AUGUSTINE N., Berlin. Republican.

GILLINGHAM, NELSON, Chester. Republican, Congregationalist, blacksmith, married; age, 57. Born in Newbury, April 4, 1835. At the age of 17 he went to Manchester to learn the machinist's trade and worked there until the panic of 1857; then went to Epping to learn the blacksmith trade. Enlisted, in 1862, in Co. A, 11th N. H. Vols., and served until the close of the war. Been residing in Chester ever since. Has served as selectman. Always a Republican.

GILMAN, ALGERNON S. A., Sandwich. Republican, Methodist, farmer, married; age, 38. Born in Sandwich, Feb. 27, 1854, and has lived for a time in Boston. Received an academic education. Has served as selectman 4 years, chairman of the board one year. Republican always.

GILMORE, GEORGE C., Manchester, Ward 4. Republican, Universalist, ex-manufacturer, married; age, 66. Born in Bedford, Sept. 25, 1826, and has resided in Portsmouth and Milford. Educated in the public and private schools and has always evinced a great aptitude for learning. Is thoroughly read and a keen observer and a close reasoner. Was colonel of the Amoskeag Veterans in 1875. He has served in both branches of the city government, and as U. S. assistant assessor four years. Member of the House in 1856-57-72-75-76-79 and 85-6; of the Senate in 1881-2, and of the Constitutional Convention in 1876. He is compiler of the "Manual of the New Hampshire Senate for the first hundred years under the Constitution," of "Roll of N. H. soldiers at the Battle of Bennington, 1777." Is president of the N. H. Society, Sons of the American Revolution, and has served as trustee of the State library since 1888.

GORDON, GEORGE H., Canaan. Republican, Baptist preference, station agent B. and M. R. R., married; age, 33. Born in Canaan, Sept. 27, 1859. Educated at Proctor Academy, Andover. Was postmaster at Danbury 5 years, and has served as town clerk of Canaan the past 5 years. Always a Republican.

GORDON, JAMES T., Concord, Ward 6. Democrat, Protestant, superintendent motive power C. and M. road, married; age, 59. Born in Meredith, Aug. 4, 1833, and has resided in Tamworth and Gilford. Enlisted in Co. A. 15th Regiment N. H. Vols., Sept. 15, 1862. Was appointed 3d sergeant and served until April 30, when he was promoted to 1st sergeant, serving in this capacity until August 13, 1863, when, his term of service having expired, was mustered out. Is a member of E. E. Sturtevant Post, G. A. R. Commenced railroading on the Boston, Concord and Montreal road in May, 1854, as a locomotive fireman; worked at this until 1856, when he entered the shop and learned the machinist's trade; commenced work for the Concord railroad as a machinist in 1865; in 1869, went out on the road as a locomotive engineer. Was appointed foreman of machine shop in April, 1873; appointed acting master mechanic August, 1878, and master mechanic June, 1879. When the Concord and Boston, Concord and Montreal railroads formed one corporation, July, 1889, was appointed superintendent of motive power, which position he holds at the present time. Is a member of Eureka Lodge of Masons; was elected master in 1870, re-elected 'in 1871. Received degrees in Trinity Chapter in 1879, in Horace Chase council in 1881. Created a Knight Templar in Mount Horeb Commandery, April, 1879. Was candidate for mayor on the Democratic ticket in 1882 and 1884.

GOSS, JOHN A., Pittsfield. Democrat. Has served as town treasurer and cashier of Pittsfield National Bank.

GOULD, MARCELLUS, Manchester, Ward 1. Republican, Congregationalist, supt. of the carding department Amoskeag Company, married; age, 47. Born in Chelsea, Vt., Dec. 20, 1845. Came to Manchester in 1864, and resided till 1871, and then for ten years in Plainfield, Conn., and has resided in Manchester the second time since 1881. Served as president of ward club 8 years, and moderator two. Member of the House in 1889, and was always a red hot Republican.

GOWING, FRED C., Dublin. Republican, Unitarian, farmer, married; age, 37. Born in Dublin, Oct. 23, 1855. Has served as selectman 3 years. Always a Republican.

GRAY, AUGUSTUS W., Bennington. Republican, Congregationalist, foreman at Goodell Company's works at Bennington, married; age, 49. Born in Bennington, May 28, 1843, and always resided there. Enlisted in Aug. 1862, in Co. D., 11th N. H. Vols.; was wounded at Fredericksburg, and mustered out in April, 1865, for disability. Is member of the G. A. R., a Mason and Odd Fellow, and the first Republican representative from his town. Has served as town clerk and moderator, and was a member of the Senate in 1889. Always a Republican.

GREEN, JAMES, Sharon. Democrat, Liberal, farmer, married; age, 44. Born in Bow, Sept. 6, 1848, and has lived in Peterboro. Served as tax collector five years and selectman seven. Always a Democrat.

GUPTILL, ERNEST L., Portsmouth, Ward 2. Democrat, Second Adventist, lawyer, single; age, 26. Born in Berwick, Me., March 9, 1866. He was born on a farm and lived there until at the age of 19; then went to Great Falls and began the study of law. Was admitted to the bar at 21 years of age. Was married at this time to Emma M. Austin of Berwick, who died one year later. He came to Portsmouth at the time of admission and has resided there since. Is active in politics, chairman of Ward 2 Democratic committee, and member of city Democratic committee. Elected city solicitor in Aug., 1891; re-elected Aug., 1892, and is also member of the board of inspectors of check-lists. Always a Democrat.

GUTTERSON, CLARENCE J., Milford. Republican.

H

HALL, CHARLES B., Walpole. Democrat; his religion is to be good and do good; farmer and runs a saw mill, married; age, 62. Born in Surry, Sept. 27, 1830, and has lived in Walpole the past 23 years. Always a Democrat.

HARRIMAN, HENRY, Madison. Republican.

HATCH, CANNING H., Northumberland. Democrat.

HATCH, OSCAR C., Littleton. Republican, Congregationalist, banker, married; age, 44. Born at Wells River, Vt; resided in Chelsea, Vt., 2 years, and in Littleton for the past 20. Educated in a private school. Has been a banker for 25 years; is president of the Littleton National Bank and secretary and treasurer of the Littleton Savings Bank. Always a Republican.

HATCH, RILEY B., Peterborough. Republican, Congregationalist, lawyer, married; age, 60. Born in Williamstown, Vt., Oct. 19, 1832. Graduated

at Middlebury College, class of 1857, and went to Peterborough as a teacher; studied law there and has resided there ever since. Has held the various town offices and was a member of the Constitutional Convention of 1889. Member of the House in 1868 and 69.

HAZELTON, GEORGE W., Hudson. Republican.

HEBERT, HENRY, Manchester. Ward 9. Always a Democrat, Catholic, hair dresser, widower; age, 37. Born at Yamaska, P. Q., May 11, 1855, and has lived in Manchester since 10 years of age. Worked in the Stark mills from 13 to 18, and has since followed his present avocation, now doing business at Hotel Merrimack, West Manchester. Served as selectman 4 years.

HILL, DANA, Chatham, Republican, farmer, and carries on a carding mill, married; age, 53. Born in Chatham and always resided there. Educated in Fryeburg, Me. Has served as chairman selectmen 6 years in succession. Always a Republican.

HILL, IRA BLAKE, Durham. Republican, farmer, married; age, 47. Born in Northwood, March 10, 1845. Educated in Strafford and Northwood.

HOBART, WILLIE A., Brookline. Democrat.

HOBBS, CHARLES W., Pelham. Democrat, Congregationalist, carpenter, surveyor and conveyancer, settles estates, and does a country justice business, married; age, 48. Born in Pelham, Nov. 5, 1844. Served as selectman 10 years, town clerk 7 in succession, and 3 since, and on the school board 5 years in all. Enlisted in the 13th N. H. Vols. when it was raised in 1862, and served with that command during its entire term of service and until the close of the war. Has been secretary of the 13th Regt. Veteran Association 4 years, but has not taken any part in G. A. R., mostly on account of there being no post in his vicinity. Never applied for a pension and is one of the very few privates of the war living. Never has taken any prominent part in politics except in his own town. Was elected representative by 55 majority, while the electors had 18 majority. Was candidate of the Democrats of Hillsborough county for register of deeds in 1892, but of course was defeated, although receiving a very complimentary vote.

HOOKE, LINCOLN FRENCH, Fremont. Republican, Universalist, farmer, single; age, 31. Born in Fremont, Jan. 12, 1861. Educated there and at Medford, Mass. Has served as selectman 4 years.

HOWARD, SAMUEL A., New Hampton. Republican.

HOWARD, TIMOTHY J., Manchester, Ward 9. Democrat, Catholic, lawyer, married; age, 30. Born in Manchester, Aug. 21, 1862, and lived 2 years in Wisconsin. Educated in the public and parochial schools of Manchester and was graduated from Laval University, Quebec. Served on school committee 2 years.

HOWE, GARDNER, S., Hinsdale. Republican, Congregationalist, merchant, married; age, 52. Born in Dover, Vt., and has lived in Hinsdale 16 years. Served as town treasurer.

HOWLAND, FRANCIS G., Lisbon. Republican, Second Adventist, farmer and produce shipper, married; age, 48. Born at Sugar Hill, Lisbon, and lived 2 years in Franconia. Educated at Sugar Hill and Newbury, Vt., seminary. Has served on the school committee and was always a Republican.

HOYT, CHARLES H., Charlestown. Democrat.

HOYT, HORACE F., Jr., Hanover. Republican, Baptist, farmer, married; age, 50. Born in Enfield, Oct. 26, 1842. Educated in the common schools. Is a son of Horace F. and Caroline E. Hoyt. His father removed to Hanover in the spring of 1843 to the district known on the map of Hanover as Hoyt Hill, where he lived till 6 years ago; was selectman in 1879, 1880, 1881, 1882 and 1883; was tax collector in 1890, 1891, 1892. Deacon of the Baptist church at Etna since 1874. Treasurer of the Etna Creamery since a short time after it was started, which is doing a $20,000 business annually. His present residence is at Etna. Has been a member

of Grafton Star grange, No. 60, since its formation fifteen years ago; elected master and has held nearly every office in the same; at present is chaplain of Mascoma Valley Pomona grange and district deputy of the fifteenth district of the state.

HUNT, ROSWELL, Piermont. Republican, Congregationalist, farmer, formerly engaged in the meat business, married; age, 64. Born in Piermont, Nov. 18, 1828, and always resided there. Educated there and in Bradford, Vt. Formerly a Whig.

HUNT, THOMAS E., Gilford. Republican, Free Baptist, farmer, married; age, 53. Born in Gilford, Sept. 5, 1839. Educated in the district schools, at Gilford academy and New Hampton Institution. Served three years in the 12th N. H. Vols. as hospital steward, enlisting as a private in Co. G, but was promoted to hospital steward before leaving the state; was on detached service much of the time, and was for nearly a year chief steward of the 18th army corps hospital located at Point of Rocks, Va.; returned with the regiment. Saw much of the horrors of war, often assisting at the amputating-table; was for a time in the drug business at Lake Village, but devoted most of his time to farming; was early connected with the grange, has been master of Mt. Belknap grange and Belknap Co. Pomona grange, and at present is deputy of district No. 4, comprising the granges in Belknap county. Served as selectman 4 years. Democrat prior to the war.

HUNTLEY, FRANK P., Claremont. Democrat, liveryman, married; age, 40. Born in Stoddard, and has lived in Marlow and Alstead. Has served as selectman.

HUNTRESS, HAMLIN, Moultonborough. Republican, postmaster and merchant.

HURLBUTT, DAVID, Dalton. Republican, farmer, married; age, 54. Born in Dalton, the youngest of 9 children. Has served as selectman 4 years and was elected representative by 31 majority in a Democratic town.

I

INGALLS, FRED W., Kingston. Democrat, physician and surgeon.

INGALLS, GEORGE H., Belmont. Democrat, hotel keeper and has served on the board of education.

J

JACKMAN, CHARLES H., Nashua, Ward 2. Republican, Congregationalist, member of the firm of C. R. Jackman and Son, wholesale and retail dealers in plumbers', steam and gas fitters' supplies, married; age, 30. Born in Nashua, July 16, 1862. Has served in the city government 3 years.

JEWELL, GEORGE E., Holderness. Democrat, merchant, married; age, 38. Born in Holderness, May 25 1854, and has always resided there. Educated there and in Nashua. Always a Democrat.

JEWETT, FREDERICK, Claremont. Republican, grocer, married; age, 65. Born in Vermont and has lived in Claremont 44 years. Has served as selectman and town treasurer. Member of the House in 1891.

JOHNSON, ALFRED F, Nashua, Ward 6. Democrat, Catholic, shoe merchant, married; age, 36. Born in Lowell, April 15, 1856, and educated there. Has served as councilman, and was always a Democrat.

JOHNSON, BENJAMIN, Epping. Democrat.

JOHNSON, DANIEL W., Claremont. Democrat.

JONES, ANDROS B., Nashua, Ward 7. Republican, foreman of shoe factory, married; age, 46. Born in Pownal, Me., Aug. 5, 1846, and lived in Stoneham and Southborough, Mass. Educated in the public schools. Has served as selectman, councilman and alderman. Was a member of the 5th and 62d Mass. Vols. in the war of the rebellion. Always a Republican.

JONES, EDWIN R., Manchester, Ward 6. Republican, attends Universalist church, early engaged in manufacturing and has been overseer of mule and ring spinning in Manchester mills since his return from the war in 1865; was married to Mary A. Farnham of Manchester and has one son, Edwin F Jones; age, 58. Born in Lebanon, Me., May 18, 1834, and with his father's family moved to Great Falls in infancy, and resided there till 1857 and since then in Manchester. Enlisted in June, 1862, in Co. A., 10th N. H. Vols., and served until mustered out, in June, 1865. Member of Louis Bell Post, G. A. R., and Mechanic Lodge, I. O. O. F. Was a Democrat before the war.

JONES, HENRY C., Rochester, Ward 4. Democrat.

K

KALEY, FRANK E., Milford. Republican, treasurer and business manager of the Morse-Kaley Mfg. Co; age, 36. Born in Canton, Mass., and began business as an office boy for the company he is still connected with. Is director of the Souhegan National Bank and president of the local building and loan association. Served on Gov. Currier's staff in 1884 with the rank of colonel. Is a Mason and Odd Fellow.

KEYES, HENRY W., Haverhill. Democrat, farmer, single; age, 28. Born in Vermont. Graduated from Harvard, class of '87. Member of the House in 1891.

KILLEY, WILLIAM E., Manchester, Ward 2. Republican.

KIMBALL, OSCAR F., Dover, Ward 1. Republican, Universalist, merchant, married; age 39. Born in Dover. Educated in her public schools and always resided there. Has served on the board of education and in the city councils. Is a prominent fraternity member, belonging to Wecohamet Lodge, No. 3. I. O. O. F., Olive Branch Lodge, No. 6, K. of P., and Wonolancet tribe, No. 7, I. O. R. M. Has been very prominently identified with the Knights of Pythias in New Hampshire. In his own lodge has held many official positions of trust, being now one of the three trustees. Has been ever active in the Grand Lodge, serving as Grand Prelate, Grand Vice Chancellor and Grand Chancellor, completing his work as Grand Chancellor in June, 1890. He closed his term very successfully instituting 8 lodges and witnessing a gain of 500 members to the order, the largest gain during any Grand Chancellor's term. Is at the present time Supreme Representative for a term of four years from Jan. 1, 1892. Always a Republican.

KINGMAN, CHARLES S., Madbury. Republican.

KITTREDGE, EVERETT, Bradford. Democrat, Episcopal preference, farmer, married; age, 42. Born in Bradford, April 26, 1850, and has lived in Warner. Educated in Warner and at New London. Served as selectman 2 years. Always a Democrat.

KNOX, JAMES E., Sanbornton. Republican, farmer and drover; age, 60. Born in Sanbornton, Nov. 6, 1832. Educated in the common school. Was one of the first to drive cattle from below Manchester to pasture in the northern part of the state and takes pride in his success as a sheep farmer. Was in poor health in the war time and was excused from service on this account. Always a Republican.

L

LAMPREY, GEORGE W., Orford. Republican, mechanic, married; age, 56. Born in Orford, June 3, 1836. Has served as town clerk. Member of the House in 1889 and 1891.

LANE, EUGENE, Pembroke. Republican, Universalist, editor and publisher of Suncook Journal, a live local weekly newspaper, married; age, 36. Born in Limerick, Me., on Christmas day, 1856. Educated in the public schools and at Limerick Academy. Lived in Augusta, Me., 6 years and for the past 12 in Suncook. Served as town clerk 2 years. Always a Republican.

LANEVILLE, DESIRE, Manchester, Ward 4. Republican, Catholic, grocer, married; age, 32. Born at Arthabaska, P. Q., Aug. 10, 1860. Came to Manchester on the day he was six years old, and resided there until 1879; then resided in Haverhill, Mass., until 1882; then returned to Manchester and has always resided there since. Is member of the Canadian Dramatic Club, and has been called an actor of no mean ability, having played in Man-

chester, Haverhill, Worcester, Nashua and other places, and has always received very high praise for an amateur. Was organizer of the Lafayette Guards, Co. H., N. H. N. G., and their first captain, which commission he resigned, business not permitting. Is a member of St. Augustin Benevolent Society; was a charter member of the Club Jolliet. His occupation has most always been that of clerk in the meat and provision stores, until the 1st of August, 1891, when he went into partnership with J. N. Lacourse, under the firm name of Lacourse and Laneville, meats and groceries. Was married, in 1879, to Miss Cordelia Lussier and has three children. Has served as councilman. Always a Republican.

LAWRENCE, FREDERICK J., Jaffrey. Republican, Congregationalist, farmer, married; age, 41. Born in Jaffrey, Oct. 13, 1851, educated there and always resided there. Served as selectman 6 years. Always a Republican.

LEACH, EDWARD GILES, Franklin. Republican, Unitarian, lawyer, married; age, 43. Born in Meredith, Jan. 28, 1849, and has resided in Franklin since 1871. Educated at Kimball Union Academy, class of '67, and Dartmouth College, class of '71. Served as county solicitor from 1880 to 84. His father, Levi Leach, and only brother, Wm. S. Leach, enlisted in the fall of '62, in Co. I, 12th N. H. Vols. His brother died in the service in Feby., '63, at the age of 16 years and 13 days. His father was discharged in 1864, from wounds received at Gettysburg. In the fall of 1864 he quit school one day at noon and went to Laconia, and tried to enlist in a company of heavy artillery with several other boys, but was prevented by his uncle, Dr. Sanborn of Franklin Falls, who saw the recruiting officers before he got there, and they rejected him. Afterwards paid his way through college by teaching school winters and as clerk at the Crawford House, White Mts., and Memphremagog House, Newport, Vt., summers. Read law with Hon. Daniel Barnard and Hon. E. B. S. Sanborn, until 1874, and was partner of the late attorney-general to 1879. Since then partner with Henry W. Stevens at Concord; is president Manufacturers and Merchants Mutual Ins. Co. of Concord, Franklin Building and Loan Association and Franklin board of trade. Also has been clerk and one of the trustees of Unitarian Society in Franklin for last past ten years, and member of the board of water commissioners of Franklin. Republican since a voter.

LEAHY, JOHN, Somersworth. Democrat, Catholic, telegraph operator, single; age, 31. Born in Somersworth, Sept. 26, 1861, educated there and always resided there. Served as supervisor 2 years. Always a Democrat.

LEAVITT, CHARLES B., Northwood. Democrat, Free Baptist, engaged in staging and express business, single; age, 46. Born in Pittsfield and is a popular and respected citizen.

LEDORX, TOUSSAINT, Nashua, Ward 3. Democrat, Catholic, machinist, married; age, 44. Born at St. Albans, Vt., Oct. 27, 1848, and has lived in Nashua 14 years. Has served as alderman 2 years.

LITTLE, SYLVESTER, Antrim. Republican.

LOCKE, JOHN E., Portsmouth, Ward 1. Democrat, overseer C. and M. railroad wharf, married; age, 57. Born in Rye, Aug. 25, 1835. Member of the House in 1891, and of the Constitutional Convention of 1889.

LOCKE, JOHN H., Carroll. Republican.

LOUGHLIN, PETER, Dover, Ward 5. Democrat, Catholic, married; age, 38. Born in Ireland and has lived in Dover since 17 years of age. He belongs to several secret societies and is very popular in his ward, having three times been elected to the House.

LOVERIN, JONATHAN L., Tilton. Democrat. Livery stable keeper.

LOVERIN, RUEL D., Croydon. Democrat, Baptist, farmer, married; age, 42. Born in Croydon, Dec. 27, 1850, educated there and always resided there. Has served as selectman and tax collector. Always a Democrat.

LUCIER, EDMOND D., Nashua, Ward 6. Democrat, Catholic, engaged in the millinery and fancy goods business, married; age, 31. Born in Nashua,, April 21, 1861, educated in her public schools and always resided there. Has served as selectman, councilman and alderman. Always a Democrat.

LYFORD, JAMES O., Concord, Ward 4. Republican, Unitarian, lawyer, married; age, 39. Born in Boston, June 28, 1853. His family removed to Canterbury when he was thirteen years of age. He has resided there, at Tilton, and at Concord since. Educated in the public schools of Boston, and at New Hamshire Conference Seminary at Tilton. Read law with Sanborn and Clark of Concord, and was admitted to the bar in 1880. Practiced law at Tilton. Elected to the Constitutional Convention of 1876 from Canterbury. Member of board of education at Tilton while residing there. Appointed bank commissioner in 1887. Has had to do with journalism since 1877, and is now an occasional editorial contributor to Republican state papers.

LYNCH, JOHN J., Manchester, Ward 5. Democrat, Catholic, book-keeper, single; age, 22. Born in Manchester Nov 19, 1870. Educated at Park street grammar school and Manchester Business College, and is the youngest member of the House.

M

MARSHALL, GILBERT A., Lancaster. Republican, Methodist preference, farmer, married; age, 41. Born in Columbia, June 27, 1851, and has lived in Lancaster 38 years. President of Farmers' League and member of board of education, and is one of the most enterprising and successful farmers in his town.

MARSTON, THOMAS F., Somersworth. Democrat, Baptist, married; age, 56. Born at Great Falls and always lived there. Member of the House in 1891.

MARTIN, ARTHUR, Plainfield. Republican.

MARTIN, DANFORTH W., Richmond. Republican.

MARTIN, JOHN F., Manchester, Ward 5. Democrat.

MATHES, GEORGE F., Wolfeboro. Republican, Unitarian, conductor on the B. and M. R. R., married; age, 36. Born in Rochester, March 25, 1856, and educated there. Member of the Constitutional Convention of 1889.

McDUFFEE, GEORGE H., Deerfield. Republican.

McDUFFEE, GEORGE W., Keene, Ward 3. Republican, Congregationalist, chair manufacturer, married; age, 51. Born in Lempster and resided for a time in Acworth. Has served as councilman and alderman.

McGREGOR, JOHN L., Whitefield. Democrat, physician and surgeon, married; age, 37. Born in Whitefield, Sept. 5, 1855, and has always resided there. Ever a Democrat.

McIVER, HENRY E., Whitefield. Republican, Presbyterian, lumber surveyor, single; age, 32. Born at Cape Breton, Feb. 29, 1860, and has lived in Whitefield 12 years. Graduated at Sydney Academy in 1878, and taught there for two terms, and then came to the grandest country on earth. Was a Liberal till he came to this country.

MEADER, STEPHEN C., Rochester, Ward 3. Republican, Friend, woolen manufacturer, married; age, 51. Born in Rochester and. educated at the Friend's school, Providence, R. I. Member of the House in 1876 and 77.

MERRICK, HENRY E., Henniker. Republican, Congregationalist, postmaster, married; age, 58. Born in Warner and educated at Henniker Academy and at New London. Went to Washington, D. C., in 1859, and was connected with the National Hotel; was chief clerk and superintendent from 1862, until 1865; was intimately acquainted with J. Wilkes Booth, he being a guest of the National at the time of the murder of Mr. Lincoln. Was one of the first witnesses at the famous trial of Mrs. Surratt and others; was employed by the war department to assist the assistant secretary of war (Gen. Eckert) in making investigations of the conspirators so far as they had connection or head quarters at said hotel; there were many of them and would often call upon Booth (he is sure

they were not all captured.) After the war was one of the proprietors of the St. Charles Hotel, Richmond, Va., until 1867. In 1871 and 1872 was manager of the Spencer Springs Hotel, Tioga Co., N. Y. Held an internal revenue appointment in. Brooklyn in 1867 and 68; census enumerator in 1880. Always a Republican.

MERRILL, CLARENCE R., Manchester, Ward 4. Republican, Universalist, flour and grain dealer, married; age, 40. Born in Norway, Me., May 12, 1852, and has lived in Manchester since 1879. Served as selectman in 1887 and 88; in common council in 1889 and 90, and assistant engineer of Manchester Fire Department from July, 1890, to the present time. Always a Republican.

MESERVE, JOHN P., Somersworth. Democrat, expressman, married; age, 47. Born in Durham.

MESKILL, JOHN, Rollinsford. Democrat.

MITCHELL, JOHN M., Concord, Ward 4. Democrat, Catholic, lawyer, married; age, 43. Born July 6, 1849. After one year old lived in Vermont until 21 years of age and then in Littleton from 1870 to 1881, and since then in Concord. Educated in the public schools of Vermont and at Derby Academy. Was supt. of schools in Salem, Vt., and member of Littleton school board and chairman of board of selectmen, 1877 and 78. Solicitor of Grafton county, 1879 to 81. State railroad commissioner from Oct. 1, 1888, to April 15, 1891. Enjoys a large legal practice and is one of the leaders of his party. Always a Democrat.

MONTPLAISIR, JOHN, Manchester, Ward 9. Democrat.

MOORE, DANIEL LOWELL, Loudon. Democrat, Adventist, farmer, married; age, 50. Born in Loudon, June 30, 1842, and has always resided there. Educated at Belmont private schools. Always a Democrat.

MORAN, JAMES H., Nashua, Ward 6. Democrat.

MORAN, WILLIAM, Portsmouth, Ward 3. Democrat.

MORRILL, FRANK I., Hopkinton. Republican, no religious preference, lumber manufacturer and dealer, married; age, 44. Born in Contoocook. Educated at New Hampton and graduated at Boston University law school in 1873, admitted to the bar in 1874 and practiced 8 years in Boston. Since 1883, has been engaged in his present business at Contoocook. Is a Mason and Odd Fellow. Served on ward and city committee in Newton, Mass., and supervisor in Hopkinton 6 years. Always a Republican.

MORRISON, GEORGE D., Marlow. Democrat, believes in the I. O. O. F. as his religion, carpenter and building mover, married; age, 54. Born in Alstead, Sept. 23, 1838. Has served as selectman, and was always a Democrat.

MORRISON, JOHN CALVIN. Boscawen. Republican. Baptist, farmer, married; age, 55. Born in Boscawen, July 18, 1837. Educated in the district schools. Has served as selectman 3 years. He calls himself a farmer but has been engaged in lumbering all his life, at times doing a large business. He has a farm of 250 acres in the Merrimack valley, raised 32 acres of corn the past season. Is wintering 54 head of horses and cattle. Is much interested in grange work and holds the office of master of Merrimack county Pomona Grange, also is chairman of the executive committee of the State Grange Fair and district deputy for the 6th district. Enlisted in the 9th N. H. Vols. and was rejected for disability. Republican always.

MORSE, FRANK O., Hebron. Democrat, believes in the religion that will do the most good to the largest number, farmer, married; age, 43. Born in Hebron, March 13, 1849. Educated in the district school, at Bristol Academy and Eastman's College, Poughkeepsie, N. Y. Has served as supervisor 11 years, town treasurer 9, and is a justice of the peace. Resides on the farm settled by his great grandfather, Dea. Jonathan Morse, on his return from the Revolutionary war, which descended to him from his father and grandfather.

MORRILL, GEORGE F., East Kingston. Democrat always, Liberal, assistant station agent and telegraph operator, married; age, 28. Born at East Kingston, April 20, 1864, and always lived there. Attended the public schools and Kingston Academy. He learned telegraphy from his brother when 12 years old, and has substituted in nearly every office from Boston to Portland. Has been in the employ of the B. and M. road since Nov. 6, 1881. Served as selectman in 1888, 89 and 90.

MOULTON, ALBERT G., Lyman. Democrat, engaged in farming and speculating, married; age, 27. Born in Lyman in 1865. Educated in Lisbon, Landaff and Tilton. Has served as selectman 3 years and town clerk 3 years. Member of the House in 1891. Democrat always.

MOULTON, ARTHUR C., Thornton. Democrat, Universalist, farmer and lumber dealer, married; age, 37. Born in Campton, but has lived in Thornton since 7 years of age. A born Democrat.

MOULTON, CHARLES B., Hampstead. Always a Republican, Universalist, shoe manufacturer, married; age, 35. Born in Hampstead, Feb. 25, 1857. As a boy he surpassed all of the same age in force of character and business ability. When fifteen years old, his father, having died, he went to Salisbury, to live with his uncle. Here he remained eight years, farming and teaming. The inducements to return to his native place being very great he came back to Hampstead in 1880, with his wife and child; for the past twelve years he has been engaged in the manufacture of shoes; and by honesty and strict attention to business he is now considered one of the most successful and prosperous young men in the town.

MOULTON, CHARLES TAPLEY, Dover, Ward 2. Republican, Congregationalist, stove and hardware dealer, married; age, 35. Born in Dover and always resided there. Educated in the public schools and Bryant and Stratton's Business College, Manchester. Served in the common council 2 years. Always a Republican.

MULLEN, JOHN P., Manchester, Ward 1. Republican, Catholic, loom fixer, married; age, 44. Born in Mayo county, Ireland, June 22, 1848. Resided in England six years and then settled in Ohio, thence removed to Massachusetts, residing 9 years in Lawrence, and has lived in Manchester 14 years. Has served 4 years as councilman. Voted for Wendell Phillips for Governor on the Greenback ticket and was active in behalf of the ten-hour law in this state.

MUZZEY, MOSES C., Sunapee. Republican, Universalist, blacksmith, married; age, 73. Born in Wendell. Educated in Sunapee. Served as lieutenant and captain in the N. H. militia.

N

NASH, JOHN B., Conway. Democrat, lawyer, married; age, 44. Born in Windham, Me., May 17, 1848, and has lived at North Conway since 1870. Served as county solicitor. Member of the Constitutional Convention of 1889, and of the House in 1891, and one of the Democratic leaders during the session.

NERBOUNE, ALFRED, Manchester, Ward 3. Republican, Catholic, carpenter, married; age, 45. Born in the Province of Quebec and has lived in Manchester 23 years, and has been employed by the Amoskeag Co. for 22 years. Belongs to several secret societies, in which he has held office, and served in the common council two years.

NESMITH, FRANK E., Surry. Republican. Has served as town treasurer.

NEWTON, SHERMAN T., Portsmouth, Ward 4. Republican, wholesale fish dealer, of the firm of Elvin Newton and Co., married; age, 28. Born at the Isles of Shoals, Sept. 5, 1864, and educated in Portsmouth. Always a Republican.

NOBLE, JOSEPH H., Nashua, Ward 6. Democrat, shoe cutter; age, 35. Born in West Kennebunk, Me., Dec. 23, 1857, and has lived in Nashua since 1884. He has served as councilman and alderman. Is an Odd Fellow and Red Man.

NOONAN, JOHN F., Gorham. Democrat, Catholic, lumber manufacturer, manager of the firm of C. S. Peabody and Co., and engaged in insurance business in Manchester since 1889, where he resided for two years, single; age, 30. Born in Gorham and educated there and at Hebron, Me., Academy. Member of the Constitutional Convention of 1889.

NORWOOD, CHARLES M., Keene. Ward 1. Democrat, box manufacturer, married; age, 48. Born in West Brookfield, Mass., Oct. 25, 1844. At the age of 12, his parents removed to Winchester, where he resided until 4 years ago. Commenced to work at the box business 30 years ago; started in business eighteen years ago last July. Removed to Keene four years ago last Oct. Employs 22 hands and makes about a million boxes per year, uses almost a million feet of lumber, and markets them in New York, Philadelphia and Baltimore. The past year he contracted to make a hundred thousand boxes for a firm, and thought that was doing well.

NOYES, ALBERT G., Epsom. Republican, Congregationalist, clerk, widower; age, 51. Born in Atkinson. At the age of 25, moved to Haverhill, Mass., and from there to Lynn, where he lived 15 years, and for the past 12 has lived in Epsom as clerk for J. B. Tennant, dealer in dry goods and groceries and general merchandise; married in Manchester, July 2, 1869, to Jennie Healey; she died Nov. 13, 1892. Has served as town treasurer.

NUTE, ALONZO IRVING, Farmington. Republican. Has served as justice of the peace, and is one of the two sons of the late ex-Congressman Alonzo Nute.

NUTTING, EBEN H., Hooksett. Republican, Methodist, agent of Hooksett Mills, married; age, 52. Born in Danville, Vt., and has lived in Manchester and Francestown, and was educated in the Manchester public and private schools and at Francestown Academy. Enlisted in Sept., 1861, in the 4th N. H. Vols., and served 3 years. Always a Republican.

NUTTER, FRANK S., Barnstead. Democrat, farmer, married; age, 37.

Born in Barnstead, Oct. 18, 1835, educated there and always resided there. Always a Democrat.

O

O'SHEA, DENNIS, Laconia. Democrat, Catholic, merchant and manufacturer, formerly member of the firm of O'Shea Brothers, married; age, 41. Born in South Ashburnham, Mass., Oct. 23, 1851, and has resided in Laconia since 6 years of age. Educated at Laconia Academy and Holy Cross College. Is proprietor of the Laconia Knitting Co., since the decease of his brother, John, two years ago, and retains an interest in the famous O'Shea store. Is an energetic, prosperous business man, and always a Democrat.

O'KEEFE, CORNELIUS, Portsmouth, Ward 1. Democrat. Member of the House in 1891.

OSBORNE, HENRY G., Rochester, Ward 2. Republican.

OSWELL, JOHN L., Berlin. Always a Republican, Lutheran, mechanic, married; age, 72. Born in Norway, Jan., 1821, and settled in Berlin in 1854. Between 1850 and 54, was leader in a political movement looking to the elevation of the laboring classes in his native country, which agitation not pleasing the government, particularly the aristocracy, made it necessary for him and others to leave to avoid arrest, which actually was the fate of all who were not successful in getting away, but who after various terms of detention were released, and sought homes also in this country. Has five sons, all staunch Republicans. One son, Sergeant Oscar N., died about two years ago from disease, the result of exposure while in the U. S. signal service. Has served as selectman.

P

PAGE, SAMUEL BERKELEY, Haverhill. Democrat, Episcopal, lawyer, single; age, 53. Born in Littleton, June 23, 1839, and has lived in Kingston, Burke, Vt., Littleton, Warren and Concord. Educated at Kingston, Lyndon, Vt., and McIndoes Falls, Vt., Academies and Law University of Albany, N. Y. Trustee of State Normal School 6 years. Member of the Constitutional

Convention of 1876. Member of the House from Warren from 1864 to 70, inclusive; Ward 6, Concord, in 1871; and from Haverhill in 1887 and 89. Always a Democrat, and is one of the keenest debaters and best parliamentarians in the State, and but few men have had his legislative experience.

PAIGE, ALBERT F., Gilmanton. Republican, Congregationalist, house and carriage painter, married; age, 51. Born at Gilmanton Iron Works. Sept. 4, 1841, and lived one year in Rochester. Enlisted in the 4th N. H. Vols., in 1861, and was in the first brigade to land on South Carolina soil after the war broke out. Was promoted for gallantry in action of May 16, 1864, and at Fort Fisher in September of the same year. Mustered out in Sept., 1865. Is prominent in Grand Army matters and is a very popular citizen.

PARKER, PERHAM, Bedford. Republican, married; age, 30. Born in Bedford, Nov. 12, 1862, on a large farm which he now owns. He does an extensive lumber business and has carried on the butchering business for the past 6 years, employing 50 or 60 men in the former. Is a very popular citizen but has never sought office. Served as constable 2 years. Brought up as a Republican.

PARKMAN, GEORGE W., Stratham. Republican, farmer, married; age, 52. Born in Palmyra, Me., Jan. 16, 1841, and educated in that state. Has served as surveyor 8 years.

PEARL, ISAAC E., Farmington. Democrat, lawyer.

PEASLEE, JOAB, Plaistow. Democrat, Universalist, farmer and wood dealer, married; age, 50. Born in Plaistow, Oct. 7, 1842. Educated at Gilmanton Academy and Phillips Exeter Academy. Went to Cincinnati, Ohio, in 1865, and taught school one year; worked for the Indianapolis, Cincinnati and Lafayette R. R. four years. Returned to Plaistow and commenced the study of law, which he was obliged to relinquish on account of throat difficulty; two years later went into a shoe manufactory in Haverhill, Mass., and worked 2 years. In 1886, quit business, his health requiring out-door exercise; built one business block and four dwellings while in Haverhill. In 1887, removed to the old homestead in Plaistow. Served as alderman in Haverhill. Always a Democrat.

PERKINS, ELIAS H., Hampton. Republican, Baptist, farmer, married; age, 50. Born in Hampton, educated there and always resided there.

PERRY, FRANCIS ALLEN, Keene, Ward 1. Republican, Unitarian, machinist, formerly master mechanic, widower; age, 61. Born in Wolfeborough, Feb. 22, 1831, and lived in Biddeford, Me.after 8 years of age and then in Boston. Has been a trustee of the Keene Savings Bank for 20 years and has served in both branches of the city government.

PERRY, HENRY E., Dover, Ward 4. Republican, Congregationalist, machinist, married; age, 43. Born in Portsmouth, Oct. 25, 1849. Learned his trade in South Newmarket in 1866, and worked there 12 years, since then has been in the employ of the Sawyer Woolen Co., mfr's of full-width, all-wool (no shoddy) goods. Served as councilman and alderman 2 years each and on the board of education 4 years. Always an active Republican.

PEVEAR, DANIEL E., Hampton Falls. Republican, Free Baptist, shoemaker, widower; age, 53. Born at Hampton Falls, Feb. 18, 1839, enlisted at the first call for volunteers and served for three years in Co. D., 3d N. H. Vols. Was discharged at Bermuda Hundred, Va., Aug. 23, 1864. Member of I. O. O. F., Rockingham Lodge, No. 22. Served as selectman 3 years.

PIERCE, FRANK E., Greenville. Republican.

PIERCE, FRED B., Chesterfield. Republican.

PIKE, HUBBARD, Stark. Republican, Methodist, farmer, single; age, 25. Born in Stark, educated there and always resided there. Has always refused public office; is vice-president of the Republican club and has always taken an active part in politics. His popularity is shown by his election in a strongly Democratic town. Always a Republican.

PIPER, JONAS W., Wolfeboro. Republican, Congregationalist, farmer, married; age, 60. Born in Wolfeboro, March 11, 1832, and always resided there. Has served as town clerk 10 years, selectman 9, and tax collector 4 years. Always a Republican.

PITMAN, GEORGE W. M., Bartlett. Democrat, lawyer, married; age, 73. Born in Bartlett, May 10, 1819. Received an academic education. Served as county commissioner and judge of probate. Member of the House 12 terms and of the Constitutional Conventions of 1850, 76, and 89.

PLUMER, CHARLES L., Alexandria. Democrat, farmer, married; age, 35. Born in Alexandria, educated there, at Bristol and New Hampton. Served as selectman 3 years. Always a Democrat.

PLUMMER, WILLIAM A., Laconia. Democrat, lawyer married; age, 27. Born in Gilmanton, Dec. 2, 1865. Educated at Gilmanton Academy, Dartmouth College and Boston University of Law. Wile at the latter institution studed law in the office of C. T. and T. H. Russell, Governor Russell being one of the members of that firm. Entered into partnership with Col S. S. Jewett of Laconia, Sept. 2, 1889, and has since been with him, and they have a very good practice indeed. Was married, Jan. 1, 1890, to Ellen F. Murray, of Canaan, daughter of G. W. Murray, Esq., with whom he also studied law. Is a Mason and member of the board of trade of Laconia. Always a Democrat.

PRESSEY, JOHN, Sutton. Democrat, Universalist, farmer, married; age, 58. Born in Sutton, Nov. 29, 1834. Attended the district and high schools until 1853, when he took a thorough course in land surveying at New London Institution under Prof. Knight, and has since done much surveying and also engaged in teaching school until the death of his father, in 1858, since which he has had the management of the homestead farm. Served on the board of supervisors for more than ten years, selectman six years, and moderator from 1880 till 1892. Always a Democrat.

PRICHARD, FRANCIS W., New Ipswich. Republican, farmer and jobber, married; age, 41. Born in New Ipswich, Feb. 14, 1851, and was in trade in Nashua two years. Educated at Appleton Academy. Served as chairman of the board of selectmen 3 years. Member of the Constitutional Convention of 1889. Always a Republican.

PRIEST, GEORGE F., Derry. Democrat, coal dealer, married; age, 46. Born in Weare.

PRIEST, HENRY P., Manchester, Ward 2. Republican.

Q

QUIMBY, FRANK P., Concord, Ward 7. Republican, chief clerk in treasurer's office, C. and M. R. R.

QUINT, SUMNER D., Manchester, Ward 3. Republican, Congregationalist, photographer, married; age, 58. Born in Orford, Oct. 26, 1834, and has lived in Marchester most of the time since 14 years old, spending two years in the South. Educated in Orford and at Highland Lake Institute, E. Andover. Has served in the city council. Always a Republican.

R

RAINVILLE, PAUL A., Somersworth. Democrat, Catholic, harness maker, married; age, 41. Born at St. David, P. Q., Aug. 15, 1851, and has resided at Great Falls since 1867. Educated in Montreal. Always a Democrat.

RANDALL, DAVID E., Seabrook. Democrat, Congregationalist, shoemaker, married; age, 56. Born in Seabrook, Aug. 1, 1836. Educated in the common schools and always resided there. Has served as selectman, tax collector and supervisor. Always a Democrat.

RAYMOND, WILLIAM H., Concord, Ward 1. Republican, Methodist, forger, married; age, 48. Born in Hopkinton, in June, 1844, and resided in Newport from 1865 to 84, and since then at Penacook, being employed by the Concord Axle Co. Enlisted at the age of 18 in the 11th N. H. Vols., and was in the 7 days siege of Fredericksburg. Reenlisted in the 20th Mass. Vols., and was severely wounded at Malvern Hill,

and taken prisoner at Hatch's Run and confined in the Pemberton prison, Richmond; was 90 days under fire. Is a member of the G. A. R., a Mason and Odd Fellow, and was always a Republican.

REED, JAMES O., Mason, Republican; age, 34. Born in New Ipswich, March 11, 1858. Has served 7 years as selectman, 4 years as chairman of the board.

REYNOLDS, JAMES A., Dover, Ward 4. Republican, Unitarian, superintendent of shoe factory, married; age, 56. Born in Durham, Nov. 7, 1836, and has lived in Madbury and Charlestown. Member of the House in 1891. Always a Republican.

RICHARDS, ALBERT L., Rochester, Ward 1. Republican, Methodist, dry and fancy goods dealer, married; age, 37. Born in Lebanon, Me., April 3, 1855, and has lived in Rochester since 1870. Educated at Lebanon Academy and commercial college in Boston. Served on the school board and member of the city council.

RICHARDSON, SAMUEL, Auburn. Democrat, mechanic, married; age, 47. Born in Londonderry, March 30, 1845, and has lived in Manchester and Michigan. Has served as supervisor and selectman.

RICKER, IRA S., New Durham. Democrat, Universalist, farmer, married; age, 68. Born in Dover, Aug. 23, 1824, and has resided in Madbury, Barrington and Melrose, and Danvers, Mass. Did not attend school much after 10 years of age, when he left home and went to South Berwick, Me., from which place he ran away and went to New Durham in 1836; ran away from there in 1839, and went to Lebanon, Me., and finally ran away from there; worked in different places and began the boot and shoe trade in 1840; got married in 1848, and since then has had no occasion to run away. Served as selectman 5 years and tax collector four. Was postmaster under Buchanan, Lincoln and Grant's administrations. Has been station agent on the B. and M. and D. and W. R. R's for 36 years. Always a Democrat.

ROBERTS, WILLIAM HALL, Rollinsford. Democrat, Baptist, lawyer in practice in Dover, single; age, 26. Born in Rollinsford, April 20, 1866. Graduated at Berwick Academy, class of '86, and Boston Law School, class of '90. Always a Democrat.

ROBIE, ELROY J., Hooksett. Republican, Universalist, concrete paver, married to Edgar H. Thompson of Webster; age, 41. Born in Hooksett, Oct. 6, 1851. Learned the blacksmith trade and worked at it 20 years, then engaged in his present business; worked in Manchester, and lived on a farm in Bow three years, and then bought out the blacksmith business of his brother, George A Robie, postmaster of Hooksett. Has served as chairman of the board of selectmen for seven years.

ROBINSON, Albert O., Wakefield. Democrat, very liberal in religious views, station agent B. and M. R. R., and agent American Express Co., married; age, 41. Born in Brookfield and received an academic education. Always a Democrat.

ROBINSON, BENJAMIN W., Manchester, Ward 4. Republican, Free Baptist, mason, married; age, 67. Born in Stratham, Jan. 1, 1826, and has lived in Manchester 48 years. Has served in the city council.

ROBY, GEORGE H., Gilford. Republican, merchant, married; age, 44. Born in Meredith, but has lived at Lakeport since 4 months old. Has been a director of the Lakeport National Bank since it was organized and is a trustee of the savings bank there. Has been in partnership with his brother in the retail boot and shoe business for 22 years, and been connected in the wood and lumber business for 15 years. Served as town treasurer.

ROGERS, FRANCIS, Dover, Ward 5. Democrat, Catholic. horse shoer, married; age, 41. Born in Dover, Oct. 31, 1851. Shipped in the U. S. navy, Sept. 25, 1864, as 2d class boy, and served 2 years; worked at horse shoeing until Oct. 5, 1869, when he enlisted in the U. S. army, and was assigned to C. troop, 4th U. S. cavalry, with which he served two years on the plains, when the regiment was ordered to Arizona and took part in the Apache war

of 1872-3-4; was discharged Oct. 5, 1874, returned to Dover, where he has since resided. Has served as councilman and alderman.

ROLLINS, ELLSWORTH H., Alton. Republican. Has served as selectman.

ROWE, JONATHAN, Newbury. Democrat, Methodist, farmer, married; age, 58. Born in Newbury, July 28, 1834, and has always resided there. Educated at New London and taught school in his earlier years. Has served on the school committee and as selectman for 5 years. Is prominent in Masonry, Odd Fellowship and the Grange. Is a tiller of the soil on the shore of Lake Sunapee and is an honored son of the Old Granite State.

ROWELL, FRANKLIN P., Newport. Republican, Congregationalist, merchant, married; age, 42. Born in Weare. Left home at the age of 18 and learned the machinist's trade in the Amoskeag shops at Manchester, after which he worked in Blood's Locomotive works, and was sexton of Franklin street church. Removed to Newport in 1874 and engaged in the grain and flour business. Started in life without a cent and says he has held his own. Educated at Francestown, and was always a Republican.

RUMERY, ALDO M., Ossipee. Democrat, Congregationalist, clerk of supreme court, married; age, 50. Born in Effingham, Oct. 10, 1842. Educated at the N. E. Masonic Institute. Has served as town clerk, selectman, member of school board, register of deeds six years, town treasurer since 1884, and his present position as clerk of courts since 1887. Always a Democrat.

S

SARGEANT, CYRUS, Plymouth. Democrat, Congregationalist, farmer, engaged in brokerage and banking in Boston, retired in 1862, and has spent much of the time since in foreign travel and study, married; age, 68. Born in Candia, Aug. 24, 1824, and went to Lowell at the age of 16, and thence to Boston, where he found employment and laid the foundation for his fortune. He was a candidate for presidential elector at the last election and was a member of the House in 1891.

SARGENT, WARREN, Allenstown. Democrat.

SCOTT, CHARLES, Peterborough. Republican. Member of the House in 1891 and took a prominent part in the work of the session.

SCOTT, WALTER WINFIELD, Dover, Ward 4. Republican, Congregationalist, law student, single; age, 25. Born in Dover, Aug. 26, 1867. Left school in 1881 to learn the engraver's trade in the Cocheco Print Works and then attended Phillips Exeter Academy. Entered the office of John Kivel, as a student, in July, 1891. Was appointed 1st sergeant of Sawyer Rifles in 1887, and commissioned captain in 1889, and major of the 1st regiment in 1892, being at the time the youngest person holding these different ranks by commission in the state. Is a Mason and secretary of the Strafford County Republican Club. Was active on the stump in the last three state campaigns. Has served as moderator and was always a Republican.

SEAVEY, JOHN E., Greenland. Democrat, Methodist, farmer, married; age, 30. Born in Greenland, Aug. 17, 1852, and always resided there. Educated there and at Hampton. Served as tax collector and chairman of the board of selectmen 3 years. A Democrat from the cradle.

SEVERANCE, CHARLES LUCIEN, Claremont. Republican, Universalist, builder, etc., married; age, 53. Born in Claremont, educated there and always resided there. Served in the 5th N. H. Vols., participated in the seige of Yorktown, battle of Fair Oaks and the 7-days' fight. Wounded at Antietam and still carries the ball in his thigh; transferred to Reserve Corps and mustered out Oct. 13, 1864. Has done much in building up the south part of the village known as "Severanceville." Served as post commander G. A. R., and on the staff of the state department commander.

SHERBURNE, JOHN D., Pittsfield. Democrat.

SINCLAIR, CHARLES A., Portsmouth, Ward 2. Democrat, Baptist preference, married; age, 44. Born in

Bethelehem, Aug. 21, 1848. Entered Dartmouth College in 1867. Is connected with several railroad corporations, as officer and director, including the Boston and Maine, Manchester and Lawrence, and Worcester, Nashua and Rochester, and with many other important business enterprises. He served on Gov. Weston's staff in 1871. Member of the House in 1873, and of the Senate in 1889 and 1891, and was the Democratic candidate for U. S. Senator at the latter session. Always an active Democrat.

SLEEPER, JAMES, Sandown. Democrat, Universalist, farmer and lumber dealer, married; age, 66. Born in Sandown and always lived there. Always a Democrat.

SMITH, AUGUSTUS W., Gilford. Republican, Protestant, employed by Wardwell Needle Co., married; age, 41. Born in Dickinson, N. Y., Sept. 14, 1851. Educated in the common school. Member of the Massachusetts Militia in 1873, and member of Co. E., 1st reg't, N. H. N. G., and served through the various grades up to lieutenant and resigned in 1881. Supervisor 4 years.

SMITH, CHARLES W., Dover, Ward 3. Republican, Free Baptist, merchant, married; age, 42. Born in Parsonsfield, Me., and has resided in So. Berwick, Biddeford and Brunswick, Me.; at the latter place was book-keeper for the Cabot Mfg. Co. for 8 years, and left it to engage in business in Dover. Educated at So. Berwick Academy. Member in 1891 and president of the common council in 1892. Past Chancellor, K. of P., and Past Grand, I. O. O. F. Always a Republican.

SMITH, GEORGE S., Manchester, Ward 6. Republican, Protestant, stock dealer, married; age, 52. Born in Chester, Dec. 15, 1840, and has resided in Manchester since 1875, and dealt quite largely in live stock, which he purchases in northern Vermont and Canada. Educated in the common school and at Pinkerton Academy. Served till the close of the war in the 18th N. H. Vols. Served as selectman and tax collector 2 years in Chester, and 2 years as councilman in Manchester. Always a Republican.

SMITH, JOHN H., Atkinson. Republican.

SMITH, ORVILLE P., Center Harbor. Democrat, Methodist preference, farmer, married; age, 31. Born in Center Harbor, March 31, 1861, and always lived there. Educated at Meredith and New Hampton. Served as chairman of selectmen 6 years, member of school board, 7.

SPOFFORD, ALDEN E., Danville. Republican.

SPRING, JOHN L., Lebanon. Republican, Congregationalist, lawyer, married; age, 62. Born in Newport, Jan. 14, 1830, and has resided in Rollinsford, Wilton and Milford. Educated in the common schools. Served as grand representative in sovereign grand lodge, I. O. O. F., 4 years, and is a Royal Arch Mason, vice-president American Bar Association. Served on school committee. Received honorary degree of A. M. from Dartmouth in 1875. Member of Constitutional Convention of 1876 and of the House in 1891. Formerly a Whig.

STACKPOLE, ALBERT T., Newmarket. Democrat.

STEVENS, DANIEL, Colebrook. Democrat, Universalist, furniture merchant, married; age, 56. Born in Warner, Oct. 8, 1836, and has lived in Colebrook since the war. Educated in the Warner common school. Served in Co. D., 1st N. H. Vols., 3 months, and then 3 years in the U. S. engineers. Was commander of Carlos Fletcher Post, G. A. R., 2 years, and delegate from Dept. of N. H. to the national encampment at Portland, Me., and has been a manufacturer and dealer in furniture for the past 14 years. Served as selectman. Always a Democrat.

STORRS, EDWARD, Hanover. Republican, Congregationalist, merchant, married; age, 50. Born in Hanover, May 18, 1842, and has lived there most of the time. Educated there and at Kimball Union Academy. Was clerk in the Hanover post-office two years from 1861; then for 3 years was engaged in telegraph and railroad work in southern Ohio. Returned to Hanover in 1866 and engaged in the dry goods and grocery business; sold out in 1872 and went to Claremont and bought the book store and jobbing business of the Claremont Stationary Co.; continued in that business for 6 years and then returned to Hanover, where he has since resided. Is now proprietor of the Dartmouth book store and senior partner in the dry goods and clothing store of Storrs and Weston. Always a Republican.

STURTEVANT, EDWARD H., Franklin. Republican, Unitarian, manufacturer of knitting machine needles, married; age, 47. Born in Craftsbury, Vt., his parents moved to Barton, and he graduated at Barton Academy at the age of 17. Taught school the following winter and the next year. Commenced to learn the drug business in Boston. At the age of 21 started a drug store in Lebanon and sold it out, and in 1868 started another in Woodstock, Vt., which he sold in 1873, and came to Franklin and purchased a drug store in each of the two villages. Sold one of them in 1875 and the other in 1889. In Jan., 1892, was one of five to organize the Franklin Needle Co. In Oct. of the same year he bought enough of the stock to make one half of the capital stock, and has since that time acted as general manager and treasurer of the Co. At the time he took the management the company was employing 30 hands; to-day it employs one hundred and seventy-five, and is crowded with orders. In Jan., 1892, when the Franklin Board of Trade was organized, was chosen one of the vice-presidents, and at the annual meeting of the Franklin Falls Co., in Feb., 1892, was chosen one of the directors and elected president. In Sept., 1892, was chosen one of the trustees of the Franklin Savings Bank, in place of Hon. Daniel Barnard, deceased. Was married in 1869 to Ada E. Martin of Colebrook; has two daughters.

SULLIVAN, FRANK, Manchester, Ward 9. Democrat.

SULLOWAY, CYRUS A., Manchester, Ward 2. Republican, lawyer, married; age, 54. Born in Grafton, June 8, 1839. Read law with Pike and Barnard in Franklin; was admitted to the bar in November, 1863, and began practice with S. D. Lord in Manchester. In 1873 he formed a partnership with E. M. Topliff, which has since continued. Served as deputy internal revenue co'lecter from 1873 to 1878. Member of the House 5 terms. He is widely known as an able lawyer and keen debater.

SWAIN, WILLIAM B., Barrington. Republican, Free Baptist, farmer and gardener, single; age, 31. Bcrn in Barrington, Aug. 23, 1861. Member of the House in 1891.

SULLIVAN, PATRICK H., Manchester, Ward 5. Democrat.

SWAZEY, CHARLES E., Bethlehem. Democrat, auctioneer.

SWEENY, PETER, Nashua, Ward 5. Democrat.

T

TALLANT, FRANK P., Concord, Ward 2. Democrat, farmer, single.

THIRIAULT, JOSEPH, Laconia. Democrat, Catholic, physician and surgeon, single; age, 32. Born in Joliette, P. Q., March 9, 1860. Entered Joliette College in 1871, graduated in 1879, was class orator. Went to Montreal to study medicine in the school of medicine and surgery, from which he graduated in 1883. Immediately moved to Ishpeming, Mich., where he practiced 10 months, and then went to Lake Linden, Mich., where he practiced until Dec., 1887. The 1st of May, 1887, he bought an interest in a drug store for $3,000, and the 21st of the same month it was totally lost in the dreadful fire which destroyed Lake Linden on that fateful day, consuming 400 houses. He had a fine practice there, and was medical officer of the board of health and secretary of La Societe St. Jean Baptiste. Owing to ill health, he gave up practicing in Dec., 1887, and came back to his Canadian home for a few months. In Nov., '88, he went to Augusta, Maine, to practice anew, and in February, 1889, came to Laconia, where he proposes to stay. Has a very good practice. Is president of La Societe St. Jean Baptiste and physician of the poor. He was a delegate to the Democratic Congressional Convention and also a member of the Democratic town committee. During the last electoral campaign he was sent by the Democratic State Committee to preach the gospel of Democracy to the Franco-American voters in several towns of the state. Always a Democrat.

TONERY, JOHN T., Manchester, Ward 5. Democrat, Catholic, cigar maker, single; age, 24. Born in Manchester, Jan. 23, 1868. Educated at Lowell and Park street schools.

TOWLE, ALAMANZOR R., Dover, Ward 3. Republican, Universalist, farmer, widower; age, 61. Born in Wolfeboro, July 31, 1831, and has lived in Dover the most of the time since 1843. Member of Olive Branch Lodge, No. 6, and Wecohamet Lodge, No. 3, I. O. O. F., Cocheco Encampment, No. 4, and North Star Lodge, Knights of Honor. Served 4 years in the common council and 2 as alderman. Always a Republican.

TOWLE, ELIAS I., Freedom. Democrat, treasurer of Ossipee Valley Ten Cent Savings Bank and merchant, firm of E. I. Towle and Co.

TUTTLE, NICHOLAS, Jefferson. Democrat, blacksmith.

U

UNDERHILL, GEORGE F., Concord, Ward 5. Republican, Unitarian, apothecary, married; age, 51. Born in Woonsocket, R. I.; educated at the Concord High School. Has held the various city offices, such as councilman and alderman. Member of N. H. commission of pharmacy and has served as secretary and treasurer of the same.

V

VAN DYKE, THOMAS H., Stewartstown. Republican. Has served as selectman.

W

WADLEIGH, MOSES, Manchester, Ward 3. Republican.

WADLEIGH, THOMAS L., Meredith. Democrat, general manager of the Meredith Shook and Lumber Co., an important enterprise employing 60 hands, married; age, 34. Born in Meredith, Oct. 21, 1858, and educated at Tilton. He has never before held political office.

WALDRON, CHARLES W., Strafford. Republican, manufacturer of lumber, married; age, 35. Born in Strafford in April, 1857, educated there and always resided there. Member of the House in 1889. Always a Republican.

WADSWORTH, DAVID, Manchester, Ward 6. Republican.

WALKER, DAVID P., Dunbarton. Democrat, Christian, farmer, married; age, 67. Born in Wilmot, Oct. 10, 1825. Educated in Wilmot and Danbury. Was selectman in Danbury 3 years and in Dunbarton one.

WALLACE, ALBERT, Rochester, Ward 6. Republican, Universalist, shoe manufacturer, single; age, 38. Born in Rochester and always lived there. Educated in Rochester, South Berwick, and Hanover.

WALLINGFORD, SAMUEL WILLARD, Milton. Republican, Congregationalist, farmer, married; age, 55. Born in Milton, Nov. 27, 1837. Made his home there until 1870, when he went to Brooklyn, N. Y., as inspector in Kings County Penitentiary from 1870 to 1878; returned to Milton in 1878 and remained there since, living on the farm and in the house where his father was born, in 1801. Served as tax collector six years. Member of the House in 1870.

WARD, LEES, Manchester, Ward 1. Republican, Universalist, loom fixer, married; age, 38. Born in Oldham, Lanchashire, Eng., Sept. 6, 1854, and came to America at the age of 3, and lived in Lawrence and Exeter before coming to Manchester. Took a prominent part in the ten-hour movement. Is a Red Man and Son of St. George. Served as selectman 2 years. Was always a Republican.

WARDWELL, GRANVILLE, Winchester. Republican, Congregationalist, commercial traveller, married; age, 55. Born in Vermont, March 4, 1837, although the home of his parents was then in Nelson. Received a common school education and has resided in Winchester since 1872. Member of the House in 1889. He has also figured as a humorous lecturer and is one of the brightest and wittiest men on the public platform. Formerly a Democrat.

WARNER, WILLIAM P., Newton. Republican, Universalist, carriage painter, married; age, 32. Born in Houlton, Me., May 22, 1860. Left home at the age of 12 to earn his own living, and landed in Portsmouth alone, and finally lived in Atkinson, Plaistow, Newton, South Hampton and Merrimac, Mass., where he learned his trade and worked at it ten years. Was prevented from entering Tufts Divinity School by ill health. Has served as supervisor and on the board of education.

WARREN, CHARLES E., Exeter. Republican.

WARREN, GEORGE M., Chichester. Democrat, Protestant, farmer, married; age, 68. Born in Epping, May 22, 1824, and has resided in Chichester since 1846. Educated in the common schools. Served as selectman 5 years and was an officer in the old state militia.

WASON, GEORGE A., New Boston. Republican, Presbyterian, farmer, married; age, 61. Born in New Boston and always resided there. Educated in her public schools and at Francestown Academy. Served as county commissioner 6 years. Member of the Senate in 1883 and of the House in 1891.

WEBSTER, CHARLES H., Enfield. Democrat, Universalist, proprietor of the Webster house and farmer, married; age, 47. Born in Enfield, March 1, 1845, educated there and always resided there. Has served as selectman, on the board of education, and as town treasurer. Was always a Democrat.

WELLINGTON, JOEL, Rindge. Republican, Congregationalist, manufacturer of wooden-ware, merchant and dealer in lumber, married; age, 61. Born in Rindge, July 7, 1831. Educated there and always resided there. Served as selectman 5 years and moderator several terms. Member of the House in 1873 and 74. Always a Republican.

WELLS, ARTHUR C., Lisbon. Republican.

WENTWORTH, WARREN G., Dummer. Democrat, farmer and lumberman, single; age, 36. Born in Dummer, Nov. 5, 1856, educated there and always lived there. Was selectman in 1891. Member of Androscoggin Lodge, No. 76, I. O. O. F. Always a Democrat.

WETHERELL, ALBERT S., Exeter. Republican, Unitarian, druggist, married; age, 41. Born in Norridgewock, Me., and educated at the Eaton school there. Served as supervisor 8 years. Always a Republican.

WHEELER, ELLERY, Shelburne. Republican, Free Baptist preference, farmer, married; age, 48. Born in Shelburne and always resided there. Educated there, at Gilead, Me., and at North Waterford, Me., high school. Served 6 months in Co. A., 17th N. H. Vols., and 10 months in Co. I., 1st N. H. H. A. Member of John E. Willis Post, No. 59, G. A. R., also of Glen Lodge, No. 54, I. O. O. F., and Gorham Lodge, No. 73, F. and A. M. Served as selectman 3 years and also as superintendent of schools. Always a Republican.

WHITAKER, WILLIAM FRANCIS, Deering. Democrat, no particular religious preference, engaged in farming and lumbering, single; age, 44. Born in Weare, July 10, 1848. Educated in the district schools and at Deering and Contoocook Academies. Served as selectman 4 years, overseer of the poor 14, tax collector 4, and town auditor 10 years. Always a Democrat.

WHITCHER, HARRY A., Warren. Democrat, engaged in teaming, married; age, 34. Born in Warren, Sept. 20, 1858. Served as town clerk 4 years, and selectman 9.

WHITCOMB, FRANK H., Keene, Ward 4. Republican, Episcopal, merchant tailor, married; age, 37. Born in Keene, Feb. 28, 1856. Educated in the public schools and at New London. Has served as councilman and alderman, being president of former body. Active in church work, 17 years member Congregational church and is now vestryman in Episcopal church. Is a prominent Mason and has held high offices in lodge and commandery. Present business was established by his father in 1863. Has done excellent literary work of a local and historical nature.

WIGGIN, GEORGE, A., Brookfield. Republican, Second Adventist, carpenter and farmer, married; age, 55. Born in Durham. Served as collector of taxes and selectman 2 years. Formerly a Freesoiler.

WIGGINS, MARTIN M., Springfield. Republican, Methodist, farmer and insurance agent, married; age, 47. Born in Springfield and always resided there. Has served as town clerk 20 years, selectman 9 years, and justice of the peace 17 years. Always a Republican.

WILEY, OSCAR H., Washington. Democrat, lumber dealer, married; age, 33. Born in Hillsboro, Dec. 28, 1859. Served as chairman board of selectmen from 1886 to 1890. Always a Democrat.

WILLARD, ZOPHAR, Harrisville. Republican, manufacturer of lumber and wooden-ware.

WILLEY, GEORGE H., Middleton. Democrat.

WINN, NATHANIEL E., Portsmouth, Ward 1. Democrat, formerly B. and M. R. R. conductor. Has served as alderman. Member of the House in 1885 and 1891.

WOODBURY, ARTHUR K., Nashua, Ward 7. Republican, Congregationalist, engaged in the roofing business and has frequently been called outside the state to do large and important jobs, married; age, 41. Born in Haverhill, Jan. 19, 1851, and has lived in Nashua since 1869. Educated in the common schools and at Haverhill Academy. Is a Mason and Odd Fellow and director of Odd Fellows' Building Association. Served as selectman and alderman. Always a Republican.

WOODBURY, CLARENCE M., Manchester, Ward 8. Republican, Universalist, overseer, married; age, 36. Born in Paxton, Mass. Has served as selectman and councilman.

WOODBURY, JAMES T., Francestown. Republican, Unitarian, farmer, married; age, 45. Born in Francestown, July 31, 1847. Educated at Francestown Academy and graduated from

Dartmouth College, class of '72, and Thayer School, class of '74. Served on the board of education, town clerk, etc.

WOODMAN, EMERY, Rye. Democrat.

WOODWARD, GEORGE, New London. Republican, merchant, married; age, 49. Born in Sutton, and educated in Lowell and New London. Has served as town clerk and treasurer. Is a notary public, and was always a Republican.

WOODWARD, JOSIAH N., Nashua, Ward 4. Republican, Congregationalist, physician and surgeon, married; age, 36. Born in East Pepperell, Mass., Sept. 6, 1856. Educated in the public schools there, in the Nashua grammar school, and two years at Harvard College. Began the study of medicine at McGill University, Montreal, and graduated from Dartmouth Medical College in 1879, and has practiced his profession in Nashua 13 years. Has served as city physician 3 years, on board of health 4 years, common council 3 years, alderman 2 years. Is a Mason, and was always a Republican.

WOODS, BENJAMIN S., Nashua, Ward 8. Republican, Baptist, grocer, married; age, 47. Born in Tyngsboro, Mass., May 28, 1845. Served 3 years in the 8th N. H. Vols., and was in all of its marches and battles. Is prominent in the G. A. R., and for 5 years was president of the 8th N. H. Veteran Association. Has been engaged in the grocery business since 1871. Was burned out in 1888. Has served in the city council, and was always a Republican.

WOODWORTH, ALBERT BINGHAM, Concord, Ward 5. Republican, Episcopal, wholesale flour and groceries merchant, married; age, 49. Born in Dorchester, April 7, 1843, and has lived in Orford, Warren, Bristol and Lisbon. Educated at Hebron and Boscawen Academy. Served as alderman two terms.

WORCESTER, JOHN R., Dover, Ward 2. Republican.

Y

YORK, FRED B., Lee. Democrat, farmer, married; age, 52. Born in Lee, June 7, 1840. Has served as selectman 8 years and in all the other offices except town clerk.

YORK, JOHN W., Kensington. Democrat, Universalist, farmer, married; age, 42. Born in Kensington, Sept. 29, 1850, and always resided there. Was liberally educated at Kingston and Hampton Academies, and has served on the school board and as town treasurer. Member of the Constitutional Convention of 1889. Always a Democrat.

YOUNG, CHARLES H., Newmarket. Democrat.

YOUNG, EDWIN J., Northfield. Republican, Baptist, married; age, 55. Born in Canterbury and has lived in Plymouth and Campton and in Northfield since 1886. Was one of the pioneers of photography, entering the business at the age of 20. Served as town clerk and treasurer in Campton. Member of the Constitutional Convention of 1889. Always a Republican.

Accidents do Happen !————————o

THE STANDARD LIFE AND ACCIDENT INS. CO.

OF DETROIT, MICHIGAN,

Will pay you for loss of time caused by accidental injuries, or will indemnify your family in case of your death from accident.

THE STANDARD	Pays full amount of its policy for the loss of both eyes, both feet or both hands, or for one hand and one foot.
THE STANDARD	Pays one third of the face of its policy for the loss of a hand or foot.
THE STANDARD	Pays one eighth of the face of its policy for the loss of one eye.
THE STANDARD	Pays the full face of its policy in case of accidental death, no matter what sums may have been previously paid for indemnity during the current policy year.
THE STANDARD	Allows 52 weeks' indemnity, while some companies allow but 26 weeks.
THE STANDARD	Has nearly $2 in assets to pay every dollar of its contract liabilities.
THE STANDARD	Has a reputation as a prompt and fair payer of all just claims.
THE STANDARD	Policies mean just what they say; it sells just what it intends to, and does deliver.
THE STANDARD	Rates are as low as a carefully tabulated experience warrants, with a small margin for profits.

READ ITS CONTRACT
LOOK AT ITS RECORD
AND YOU WILL BUY AND CARRY ITS POLICY

H. B. BROWN, Agent,
CONCORD, N. H.

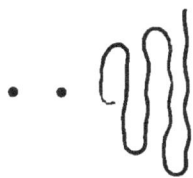